PRAISE FOR *The Automatic Millionaire*

"*The Automatic Millionaire* is an automatic winner. David Bach really cares about you: On every page you can hear him cheering you on to financial fitness. No matter who you are or what your income is, you can benefit from this easy-to-apply program. Do it now. You and your loved ones deserve big bucks!"

—Ken Blanchard, coauthor of
The One Minute Manager®

"*The Automatic Millionaire* gives you, step by step, everything you need to secure your financial future. When you do it David Bach's way, failure is not an option."

—Jean Chatzky, financial editor, NBC's *Today*

"Finally, a book that helps you stop sweating it when it comes to your money! *The Automatic Millionaire* is a fast, easy read that gets you to take action. David Bach is the money coach to trust year in and year out to motivate you financially."

—Richard Carlson, author of *Don't Sweat the Small Stuff*
and *Don't Sweat the Small Stuff About Money*

"David Bach's *The Automatic Millionaire* proves that you don't have to make a lot of money or have a complicated financial plan to get started—you can literally start toward your financial dreams today, in a matter of hours, with just one life-changing secret: Pay yourself first and make it automatic! Equally important, this book shows you how to simplify and automate your entire financial life."

—Harry S. Dent, Jr., investment strategist and author of *The Roaring 2000s*

"*The Automatic Millionaire* is, simply put . . . a great little book! You can read it in a matter of hours and take action immediately on a powerful, simple, totally AUTOMATIC plan to become a millionaire."

—Robert G. Allen, coauthor of *The One-Minute Millionaire*

"David Bach makes understanding your finances easy, fun, and exciting. *The Automatic Millionaire* is a practical and smart guide to mastering your relationship with money."
—Barbara De Angelis, Ph.D., author of *What Women Want Men to Know*

"More people will become millionaires in the years ahead than in all the previous years of human history. It has never been more possible for you to get out of debt, achieve financial independence, and build a financial fortress around yourself than it is today. This fast-moving book by David Bach gives you the practical strategies and techniques you need to take complete control of your financial life and become the millionaire you want to be."
—Brian Tracy, author of *Goals!*

"David Bach lets you in on the secret to finishing rich, and it's so simple anyone can do it. Read this book, follow his advice, and it will change your life."
—Candace Bahr and Ginita Wall, cofounders of the Women's Institute for Financial Education (WIFE.org)

"Pay yourself first. It's simple ideas like this that can make all the difference in your financial future. Ignore David Bach's new book at your own peril."
—Al Ries, author of *Focus: The Future of Your Company Depends on It*

"*The Automatic Millionaire* is brilliant in its simplicity and thoroughly enjoyable to read. If you want to create financial security and still sleep at night, you've just got to get this book! Thank you, David . . . your advice will change people's lives."
—Barbara Stanny, author of *Secrets of Six-Figure Women* and *Prince Charming Isn't Coming*

"I once heard that to make something powerful, you need to make it practical. *The Automatic Millionaire* is a book that is 100% practical and powerful. David Bach is one of the few individuals in the world of finances who truly want to make a huge impact in other people's financial lives. This is one of those rare books that can really change your life!"
—Louis Barajas, author of *The Latino Journey to Financial Greatness*

PRAISE FOR *Smart Women Finish Rich* and *Smart Couples Finish Rich*

"*Smart Couples Finish Rich* teaches women and men to work together as a team when it comes to money. Bach's nine steps are powerful, yet easy to understand and fun to implement. The entire family can benefit from this great book."
—Robert T. Kiyosaki, author of *Rich Dad, Poor Dad*

"David Bach is the one expert to listen to when you're intimidated by your finances. His easy-to-understand program will show you how to afford your dreams."
—Anthony Robbins, author of *Awaken the Giant Within* and *Unlimited Power*

"I know how hard it is to make a personal-finance book user-friendly. Bach has done it. *Smart Couples Finish Rich* picks up where *Smart Women Finish Rich* left off. . . . This is an easy, lively read filled with tips that made me smile and at least once made me laugh."
—*USA Weekend*

"*Smart Couples Finish Rich* is a must-read for couples. Bach is a great financial coach . . . he knows how to bring couples together on a topic that often divides them."
—John Gray, author of *Men Are From Mars, Women Are From Venus*

"*Finally* a book for women that talks about money in a way that makes sense. David Bach is not just an expert in managing money—he's the ultimate motivational coach for women. I can't recommend this book enough. It's a must-read!"
—Barbara De Angelis, Ph.D., bestselling author of *Real Moments*

"[David] Bach gets across some complicated stuff: how to organize a portfolio, keep the taxman at bay, invest in yourself, and earn more, all of which make this book one of the best overall."
—*Working Woman*

THE
AUTOMATIC
MILLIONAIRE
WORKBOOK

Also by David Bach

Smart Women Finish Rich®

Smart Couples Finish Rich®

The Finish Rich Workbook

1001 Financial Words You Need to Know

The Automatic Millionaire®

Start Late, Finish Rich

THE
AUTOMATIC
MILLIONAIRE
WORKBOOK

A Personalized Plan
to Live and Finish Rich

DAVID BACH

BROADWAY BOOKS   New York

BROADWAY

PRINTED IN THE UNITED STATES OF AMERICA

BROADWAY BOOKS and its logo, a letter B bisected on the diagonal,
are trademarks of Random House, Inc.

Visit our web site at www.broadwaybooks.com

First edition published 2005

ISBN 0-7679-1948-3

3 5 7 9 10 8 6 4 2

To the millions of readers of *The Automatic Millionaire* and the thousands who have written to me.

Thank you for your feedback, encouragement, letters and e-mails, and success stories.

You inspire me to do what I do.

CONTENTS

INTRODUCTION

Thank you for picking up a copy of this book and congratulations on choosing to create an easier financial future! *The Automatic Millionaire Workbook*, which you hold in your hands, is based on the international best-selling book *The Automatic Millionaire*.

If you've already read *The Automatic Millionaire*, welcome back. As I'm writing this, *The Automatic Millionaire* is approaching one million copies in print around the world and has been translated into seven languages. I've had the incredible privilege of sharing the ideas of the "Automatic Millionaire Philosophy" on *The Oprah Winfrey Show*, NBC's *Today* show, CNN's *American Morning*, and many other television shows, and in a very short period many people from all walks of life and income levels have been helped by the simple and powerful message. The success of this little book has been exciting and humbling—as I've seen firsthand how great a need there is for simple, actionable coaching on money. My dream with *The Automatic Millionaire* was to create a book you could read in less than an hour and a half and implement the plan in less than sixty minutes. As you'll see, based on many of the success stories of readers in this book, it's clearly working.

So why write a workbook? Why create a companion guide to *The Automatic Millionaire*? For starters, many of my readers (maybe you) have written to me asking for it. Second, I've written this companion guide to help my readers take the incredibly simple wealth-building plan I laid out in *The Automatic Millionaire* and bring their knowledge to the next level. Having had the opportunity to coach millions of people around the world on how to live and finish rich, I've seen firsthand that when people write things out, they learn the material better and follow through on their plans more often.

My goal with *The Automatic Millionaire Workbook* is to help you create a simple, complete, step-by-step plan that will make you a millionaire by the time you retire—and help you retire earlier than you ever thought possible.

IN FIVE QUESTIONS, I CAN TELL IF YOU'LL BE A MILLIONAIRE

In the past few years, thousands of people have asked me, "David, what's the secret to being rich?" In talking with them, I've discovered that the *only* difference between millionaires and the people who spend their lives living paycheck to paycheck is this: **The millionaires know the strategies that work and follow them.**

So I came up with a simple test to find out which people knew the strategies and which ones didn't. Now I can say with confidence:

I can ask you five questions and know with 90% accuracy if you'll be a millionaire.

It's that simple. The questions are very straightforward; answering all five takes about three minutes. But they reveal everything about your financial prospects.

The Five Questions:
1. Do you know your Latte Factor?
2. Do you "Pay Yourself First"?
3. Have you made your financial plan automatic?
4. Do you own your home?
5. Do you tithe?

If you answer "Yes" to all five questions, based on my experience you've got an *excellent* opportunity to become a millionaire.

How do you answer the Five Questions now? How would you like to answer them by the time you're finished with the workbook?

LEARN IT. WRITE IT. LIVE IT.

This book is filled with exercises based on *The Automatic Millionaire*, but taken several steps further. The exercises give you the tools you need to turn the ideas from that book into concrete plans you can put into action *today*. Every step of the way, I will guide you through the concept; then the exercises will make it personal by showing you how you can apply the concept to your life. Again, I've found from experience—both in coaching others and my own life—that if you write something down, you're much more likely to follow through. I want you to follow through! I've also given you blank pages titled "Brainstorming Breaks," where you can answer some important questions about your finances and your lifestyle in any way you like. Use the "Brainstorming Breaks" as a journal. This is your place to get down on paper the thoughts that are in your head and heart.

And I will share some real-life success stories from readers who are living the Automatic Millionaire dream. These stories are fantastic teachers. Nothing proves the value of what I'm talking about better than real people talking about how the things they've learned have changed their lives. I hope you enjoy them and they inspire you to take action.

WHO STOLE THE AMERICAN DREAM?

Once there was a country where people went to work for a company, were paid well, bought a house, raised a couple of kids, and put money into a company retirement plan. If they stayed at the company for 30 or 40 years, they retired with a gold watch, a pension, and lived happily ever after.

Unfortunately, today the American Dream is on life support. Companies are outsourcing and downsizing, the company pension is one of those things we talk about by saying, "Remember when?," and let's not even get started about Social Security.

At the same time that our jobs are becoming more uncertain, we're spending more and saving less. Thanks to our consumer culture, the average American household is carrying $18,700 in consumer debt! Nearly 60 million Americans have not a single dollar saved for their retirement. Even the typical baby boomer, supposedly part of the wealthiest generation in history, has less than $10,000 in assets saved. According to a recent AARP (American Association of Retired Persons) study, only one in five baby boomers has more than $25,000 in savings. Recently, I conducted my own Finish Rich survey with researchers at Temple University for a new book called *Start Late, Finish Rich*. Our survey found that three in ten had less than $1,000 in savings and 70% of respondents were living paycheck to paycheck.

MY FREE GIFT TO YOU

To read a free excerpt from my new book *Start Late, Finish Rich*, visit **www.finishrich. com**. We also posted a free audio download called *The Automatic Millionaire Jump Start Program* and a new audio on *Start Late, Finish Rich*. Both are available free to you—so enjoy!

The unfortunate bottom line to wealth in America is that we often spend everything we earn . . . and a lot more.

IT DOESN'T HAVE TO BE THAT WAY

Those numbers mean that for millions of Americans, retirement will never be an option. They'll have to go on working into their sixties and seventies, living paycheck to paycheck, bill to bill.

I think that's a tragedy. But the saddest part is that 90% of those future "unretirees" make enough money *right now* to become millionaires—if they knew what to do. And here's the thing: *So do you*. You may not believe it right now, but you will by the time you finish this book. You will learn how to reclaim the American Dream for yourself and your family.

WHAT EXACTLY IS THE AMERICAN DREAM?

Take a moment to think about what that really means to you. Write out in the Brainstorming Break right now what you think the American Dream is— being as specific as possible.

BRAINSTORMING BREAK

What's your idea of the American Dream?

EXERCISE
The American Dream Snapshot

Chances are, in your brainstorming session you realized that becoming an Automatic Millionaire isn't just about the money; it's about leading the kind of life you want. The American Dream Snapshot will help you bring that life into focus.

How to use it: In the first column, write down the three most important parts of your American Dream. They could be sailing around the world, starting a business, sending your kids to college, buying your first home. There are no "right answers"—*only your honest answers matter*. Write down what you want most. In the second column, take your best guess at how much money you'll need to make each part of your dream a reality. And in the last column, explain why each dream is important to you.

THE AMERICAN DREAM SNAPSHOT		
What Are Your Top Three American Dreams?		
What Do You Want?	**What Will It Take?**	**Why Is It Important?**
Example: "To own my own home."	*Example: "A $40,000 down payment and a clear credit history."*	*Example: "I want the security and pride that comes with owning my own home."*
1		
2		
3		

When you've finished the exercise: Knowing your dreams is the first step toward setting real, definable goals that will make your life completely fulfilling. This is a great start.

THE SECRET TO LIVING THE AMERICAN DREAM

I decided to write *The Automatic Millionaire* and this companion workbook because after my radio and TV appearances, book signings and seminars, people were asking me the same question: *"David, what's the one thing I need to do to get rich? Can I still do it, or have I missed out?"*

Even my friends ask me this. So I decided to write these books to share the secret with the millions of people who should be living the American Dream—and can, if they follow one simple step.

There actually *is* one incredibly simple secret to getting rich in America. It's so simple that almost no one does it. Everybody's busy looking for complex solutions that sound good on Wall Street, but that's not where the answers are.

The secret to becoming a millionaire is powerfully simple:

Make your financial plan automatic.

By making your plan automatic, you don't need discipline or to remember to write checks every month. You don't need a lot of money. All you need to do is take full advantage of the technology that lets you make automatic monthly payments to everything from your mortgage to your 401(k) without lifting a finger.

If you want to get rich, make it so you don't have to think about it! Behind the scenes, as you go about your daily life, your debt will be shrinking, you'll be getting closer to owning your home, and you'll be building assets that will give you the freedom to make your American Dream a reality.

WHAT'S HOLDING YOU BACK?

Money isn't why people fail to reach their financial goals. You almost certainly make enough money *today* to become an Automatic Millionaire. So what's the reason?

The biggest reason people fail is that they often lie to the world and to themselves about their financial situation. They lie to the world by living beyond their means so other people will think they "have it all." They are the people you see driving a new car and wearing a fancy watch—but they rent, have $20,000 in credit card debt, and live paycheck to paycheck. Then they lie to themselves by promising that "this time" they'll pay all their bills in full. Instead, the debts just grow and grow. Then they feel bad, and the cycle of financial lies continues and gets deeper and deeper. This is what I call *"leasing your lifestyle instead of owning it."*

To become an Automatic Millionaire, you must *tell yourself the truth* about money. Your actions need to reflect who you are—so that you can become who you really want to be. The truth is that all financial progress, both yours and mine, ultimately comes from telling the truth about our current situation. Are you ready? Let's get started.

EXERCISE
The Automatic Millionaire Truth Tester

How to use it: In the first column, you'll see a list of financial habits that can damage your chances of being an Automatic Millionaire. In the second column, write "true" if you're guilty of the habit and "false" if you're not. In the last column, write down what you can do to change your bad habits.

THE AUTOMATIC MILLIONAIRE TRUTH TESTER		
Habit	True or False?	What Can I Do to Change It?
Example: I use credit cards for purchases instead of paying cash.	*True*	*Stop taking credit cards with me when I shop and start saving cash for the things I want to buy.*
I buy things I can't afford to impress my friends.		
I often spend "some" of my paycheck before I even get it.		
I shop for fun, not because I need to.		
I say "yes" to new credit card offers.		
I only pay the minimum on my credit cards.		
I'm often late with my credit card payments.		
I don't balance my checkbook or check bank statements.		
I promise to save money every month, but don't.		
I don't save anything toward a down payment on a home.		
I put money aside for future emergencies, and I end up spending it.		

When you've finished the exercise: OK, so you're not perfect. Nobody is. That's not the point. The point is to *understand* how your bad habits affect your financial future so you can take steps to change them. And you're already doing that, so bravo.

A FINANCIAL PLAN BASED ON YOUR VALUES IS ALWAYS A WINNER

In addition to telling yourself and the world the "truth" about your financial situation by living a life congruent with your financial ability, there's another kind of truth you need to tell yourself—your values, what's truly important to you. The journey of any successful Automatic Millionaire begins not with money but with *values*.

The purpose of becoming an Automatic Millionaire isn't to accumulate money for its own sake. It's to achieve *freedom*—freedom that allows you to do the things that give your life meaning. Remember:

Every financial decision should be driven by what you value.

JIM AND SUE'S VALUES

Jim and Sue McIntyre were a perfect example of this. They were the first Automatic Millionaires, and you'll be reading more about them in the next chapter. When they came into my office, Jim told me his parents had worked almost all their lives. "One of my core values was that I wanted to achieve security for my family and freedom for myself," he said. Jim wanted to spend the second half of his life doing what he wanted when he wanted.

Sue wanted to know that her two children would always be safe, but she also wanted to be able to remain a part of their close-knit community. Jim and Sue and their neighbors were incredibly close; they would all mow their lawns at the same time each weekend so they could socialize! One of Jim and Sue's goals was to retire early with the rest of their friends.

So they set up a financial plan keyed to those values, and you know what? Jim and Sue did retire early (as did many of their neighbors), and they were able to give their family the financial security they desired.

EXERCISE
The Values Conversation

When I appeared on *The Oprah Winfrey Show*, the producers asked me to work with some couples from the audience who were fighting about money. I had the couples sit down, draw a circle, divide it into six slices, write one core value in each slice, and then talk about each value. I called it the Values Conversation. It worked wonders; once these people understood the values they shared, it was easier for them to agree on the goals they wanted to reach and the actions they needed to take.

You see, values are the things that are important to you personally, things that might have nothing to do with money, like security, freedom, and faith. Goals are specific things you want to achieve, such as owning your home, taking an annual vacation, or giving to a church. Your values should always drive your goals, not the other way around.

So we're going to have our own Values Conversation.

How to use it: If it's just you, write your core values for life in the six circle slices. If you have a partner, take turns, writing three values each. Then talk about them. Why do you hold those values? Are there values that you and your partner share?

THE VALUES CONVERSATION—JIM AND SUE'S VALUES

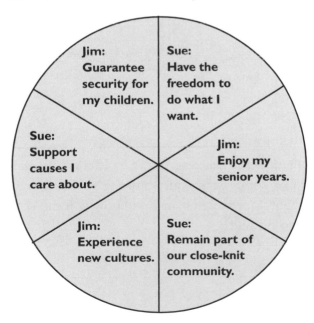

THE VALUES CONVERSATION—YOUR VALUES

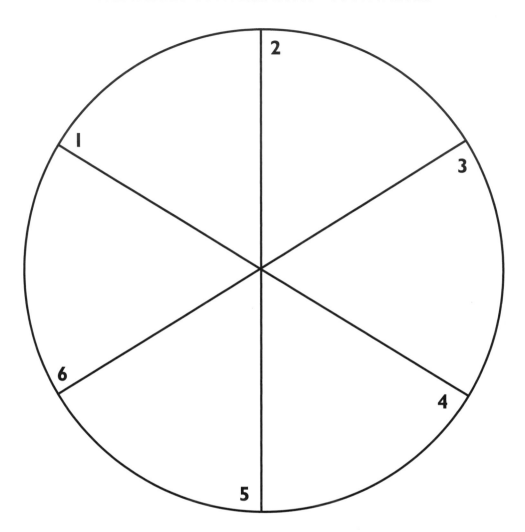

When you've finished the exercise: You've looked at your American Dreams. Your dreams should come from your values. Use this exercise as a starting point for a talk about your shared values and how you can change your financial life to serve those values.

BRAINSTORMING BREAK

What did you learn about your values?
Were there any surprises?

VALUES ARE THE SEEDS OF GOALS

Every financial goal and decision you make should be based on your values. In the next exercise, you will see how your goals grow out of your values. And then I will ask you to figure out how much money each goal will take.

A few people have told me that equating goals to money is silly if you don't have any money. I disagree. Doing most things in this world takes money—and if you don't know what it costs, you can't create a realistic plan to make it happen. If one of your core values is to help your children have a better life than you and one of your goals is to provide them with a world-class education, you need to know how much money private school and an Ivy league education will cost. This is very basic Automatic Millionaire math:

$$Goals = Values \times Money$$

Figuring out how much money you'll need to reach your life's goals will make them more real. Then you'll be more able to map out the steps—financial and otherwise—you need to take to reach each goal.

> ### EXERCISE
> ## The Automatic Millionaire Goal Developer

How to use it: In the first column, write your six core values from the Values Conversation. In the second, write down the goals you think you'll need to reach to serve each value. In the last column, write down how much money it will take to reach each of those goals.

THE AUTOMATIC MILLIONAIRE GOAL DEVELOPER		
My Values	**My Goals**	**How Much Money I'll Need**
Example: Retire with financial security	*Pay off mortgage early*	$123,500
	Pay off consumer debt	$23,432
1		
2		
3		
4		
5		
6		

When you've finished the exercise: There's a saying that goes, "A goal is a dream with a deadline." Well, first you looked at your dreams, then your values. Now you know what you need to do to reach your goals. I'd say you're ready for action.

"OK, NOW I KNOW WHERE I'M HEADED. WHAT'S NEXT?"

The next chapter will introduce you to the original Automatic Millionaires, and the chapters that follow will help you put a plan in place so you, too, can finish rich.

But before you plunge ahead, I've got two more things to share with you. At the end of each chapter, you'll find a Motivator—a tool that lets you recap what you learned from the chapter and write down a step-by-step plan for putting your new knowledge into action. As soon as you finish each chapter, fill out the Motivator right away, while what you've learned is still fresh in your mind.

And at the end of the workbook you'll find the Power Charge Worksheets™, a chapter-by-chapter journal where you can keep track of everything you do to get your Automatic Millionaire plan up to speed. Each time you take a positive step—setting up automatic payroll deduction for your 401(k), for example—record it in the Power Charge. Then, each time you come back to the workbook, take a look at your Power Charge first. You'll get really fired up seeing all the progress you've made! You'll find these worksheets on pages 187–94.

IS IT TOO LATE TO BECOME WEALTHY? ONLY IF YOU WAIT.

You have a household income of $60,000 a year, a mortgage, $12,000 in credit card debt, two kids, no savings, and you have no idea where your money goes every month. Can you still become a millionaire by the time you retire?

Yes—if you take action *now* to get organized and automate your financial plan. That's what we're going to do in *The Automatic Millionaire Workbook*. Together, we're going to walk through every step you'll need to take to put your finances on autopilot.

If you learn and live by the philosophy of the Automatic Millionaire, you can build a life of almost unlimited financial promise.

THE PHILOSOPHY OF THE AUTOMATIC MILLIONAIRE

- You don't have to make a lot of money to be rich.
- You don't need discipline.
- You don't need to be self-employed.
- You can build a fortune on a few dollars a day.
- The rich get (and stay) rich because they pay themselves first.
- Homeowners get rich. Renters stay poor.
- You need an automatic system so you can't fail.

I'm going to show you how you can make all those things happen in a few hours, with a few phone calls and a few mouse clicks. It's simple and incredibly rewarding. With your automatic plan in place, you can enjoy life, free of worries about money.

It really can be done. As you'll see, if Jim and Sue McIntyre can become Automatic Millionaires, you can, too. Ready? Let's get started!

CHAPTER ONE

MEETING THE AUTOMATIC MILLIONAIRE

THE WORLD'S MOST UNEXPECTED MILLIONAIRES

Jim and Sue McIntyre were the first Automatic Millionaires I ever met. Jim and Sue came into my office bubbling with excitement at the idea of Jim's early retirement at age 52. Often, married couples would ask to meet with me to talk about what they needed to do to retire early. Usually, I had to tell these lovely people they weren't going to be able to retire when they hoped to. I looked at Jim and Sue McIntyre—a middle manager at a utility company and his beautician wife, with a very average combined income of $55,000— and I assumed I would be giving them the same kind of bad news.

"THE MCINTYRES DON'T DO DEBT."

Fortunately, I couldn't have been more wrong. Jim passed over a folder of documents detailing income, assets, and debts. I flipped through them, and something stopped me cold.

AN AUTOMATIC MILLIONAIRE SUCCESS STORY

One week after I finished *The Automatic Millionaire*, I started a Roth IRA, consolidated my credit card debt to another card, began saving 8% of my income, and took my income tax refund and split it four ways—saved 25%, put 25% into a CD, used 25% (to pay off my credit card), and added 25% into my IRA.

I will soon be debt-free, have savings, and have some investments. Thank you for not only writing *The Automatic Millionaire*, but for making it so simple that anyone can understand and learn from it.

Anthony Valerius
Nutley, NJ

"You have no debt?" I asked them. Sue chuckled and said, "The McIntyres don't do debt." I kept going through their financial records. They owned the house they lived in and an income property, and both mortgages were paid. Jim had a 401(k) worth $610,000, and Sue had two retirement accounts worth $72,000. They had more than $220,000 in additional assets in cash and bonds. Add their boat and three cars (all paid for) and some other personal property, and Jim and Sue had a net worth near $2 million, plus over $26,000 a year in rent from their income property, and Jim was eligible for a small pension.

This "ordinary" couple had a seven-figure net worth, no debt, a huge nest egg, and several streams of income. No wonder they were giddy at the prospect of early retirement!

EXERCISE
The Automatic Millionaire Scorecard

Jim and Sue McIntyre have achieved financial goals that most Americans only dream of: owning their home, owning an income property, retiring early with peace of mind. I'd like you to ask yourself what you want from your retirement. Have you started taking steps to reach those goals? Decide what you want today and you can take real steps to make it happen.

How to use it: Look at the retirement "wants" in the first column. In the second column, write a "Y" for each item if you want that in retirement, "N" if you don't care. Then, in the third column, circle the number that tells how close you are to reaching each goal. For example, if your house is 90% paid off, check 9 for "A paid mortgage." But if you don't even own a home yet, check 1.

THE AUTOMATIC MILLIONAIRE SCORECARD		
What You Want	**Y/N**	**How Close? 10 = Achieved It, 1 = Not Begun**
Buy a home		(circle one) 1 2 3 4 5 6 7 8 9 10
Pay off my mortgage		(circle one) 1 2 3 4 5 6 7 8 9 10
A vacation home		(circle one) 1 2 3 4 5 6 7 8 9 10
Long-term care coverage		(circle one) 1 2 3 4 5 6 7 8 9 10
Boat or RV		(circle one) 1 2 3 4 5 6 7 8 9 10
Rainy day account		(circle one) 1 2 3 4 5 6 7 8 9 10
Start a business		(circle one) 1 2 3 4 5 6 7 8 9 10
Volunteer		(circle one) 1 2 3 4 5 6 7 8 9 10
Donate to a cause		(circle one) 1 2 3 4 5 6 7 8 9 10
Go back to school		(circle one) 1 2 3 4 5 6 7 8 9 10
Own income property		(circle one) 1 2 3 4 5 6 7 8 9 10
(write your own)		(circle one) 1 2 3 4 5 6 7 8 9 10

When you've finished the exercise: What did you learn about what you want from your retirement? What can you do today that will get you closer to having the things you want? Keep reading, and Jim and Sue McIntyre will inspire you.

WHAT DO YOU OWN AND OWE?

Jim and Sue are unusual, I think you'll agree. Not many people with their incomes own such an impressive list of assets, all free and clear. In fact, most Americans owe far more than they own.

But it doesn't have to be like that for you. You can take control of your financial life like the McIntyres and become an Automatic Millionaire, with a net-worth statement that inspires others. Let's start by figuring out what *you* own and owe today.

EXERCISE
The Automatic Millionaire Balance Sheet

It's a real eye-opener to add up how much you're really worth. If you own a home, I think you'll be pleasantly surprised at how high your net worth truly is!

How to use it: In the Assets column, write down the value of all the things you own. In the Liabilities column, write down what you owe on all your debts. Add both columns, then subtract the Liabilities from Assets, and write the result down in the Net Worth box.

THE AUTOMATIC MILLIONAIRE BALANCE SHEET			
Assets		**Liabilities**	
Real estate (home)	$	Real estate mortgage (home)	$
Real estate (rental)	$	Real estate mortgage (rental)	$
Cash savings	$	Student loans	$
401(k)	$	Credit cards	$
IRAs	$	Personal loans	$
Stocks/Mutual funds/CD	$	Liability (business)	$
Bonds	$	Bank loan, equity line, etc.	$
Business	$	Car loans	$
Personal property (car, boat)	$	Other loans	$
	$		$
	$		$
	$		$
	$		$
	$		$
	$		$
	$		$
Total Assets	$	**Total Liabilities**	$
Net Worth (Total Assets Minus Total Liabilities)			$

When you've finished the exercise: Now that you have your liabilities written out in black and white, ask yourself—what can you do today to reduce them? Now let's get back to Jim and Sue.

"WE DECIDED TO PAY OURSELVES FIRST."

I was fascinated by how the McIntyres had built such a significant net worth for themselves. They looked so . . . typical. "How did you do this?" I asked them. Jim and Sue told me they had tried budgets and ended up just fighting about money. So, early in their married life, they made a decision: Instead of living paycheck to paycheck, they would make their money work for them.

"Most people think that when they get their paycheck, the first thing they should do is pay their bills, and then if there is anything left over, save a few dollars," Jim told me. "Our parents taught us that to really get ahead of the game, you have to turn this around. Put aside a few dollars for yourself, *then* pay all your bills." In other words, *pay yourself first.*

AN AUTOMATIC MILLIONAIRE SUCCESS STORY

When I began my job last fall, the first thing I did was to max out my 403(b), which came to 22% of my annual income. My employer began contributing 10% of my base income from day one. I also decided to use part of my extra summer income to max out my IRA contributions. Because this planning and saving was such a rush, I began putting another 7% of my monthly income into automatically deducted taxable investments (stocks, bonds, and CDs). Then I began adding 10% to my mortgage payment. I felt that I was not only financially in control, but that I was finally focusing on money as part of my greater personal value system. . . . It is six months since I began my job, and at the age of 28, I know that I will never worry about money. Sure, sometimes my extra spending money seems a bit tight, but I just take out my (financial) inventory, think about my values, and head to the library or the dollar theater. Thank you, David, for *The Automatic Millionaire* and for giving me control over my life!

Dr. Ali Bryant
Bloomington, IN

Jim and Sue had started setting aside part of their incomes before taxes were taken out and putting the money into savings and investments. Since they couldn't see the money, they didn't miss it. It just piled up and grew into a pretty substantial amount. The McIntyres started by setting aside just 4% of their incomes, and when we met, they were saving 15%.

What a simple, brilliant idea. It started me thinking about all the people who were creating budgets and fighting about money. They had it all backward! **All you had to do was pay yourself first, and you didn't need a budget!**

In this next exercise, we're going to start by doing it backward. We're going to figure out exactly what you're making and spending, and what's left at the end of each month. Then, later in *The Automatic Millionaire Workbook*, we'll turn the tables and have you figure out how much you can Pay Yourself First!

EXERCISE
The Automatic Millionaire Income Statement

This exercise will make very clear how paying everyone before you pay yourself leaves you with so little to save.

How to use it: Write down everything you bring home each month from every source of income, before taxes. Then write down all your monthly expenses, including taxes. Add 10% to your expenses for the Murphy's Law Factor, because there are always unexpected expenses. Then subtract expenses from income and voilà! You have your Net Cash Flow—the money you can save.

THE AUTOMATIC MILLIONAIRE WORKBOOK

THE AUTOMATIC MILLIONAIRE INCOME STATEMENT

Income / How Much You Earn Per Month

Salary: Wages, tips, commissions, self-employment income	$
Interest Income	$
Dividends	$
Rental Property	$
Trust Accounts	$
Alimony, Child Support, Widow's Benefits	$
Social Security Benefits	$
Business Income	$
Other Income	$
Total Income	$

Expenses / How Much You Spend Per Month

Type	Description	$
Taxes	Federal, State, FICA, Property Taxes	$
Housing	Home Mortgage Payments, Utilities, Insurance, Repairs, Cleaning Services, TV/Cable, Home/Cell Phone, Landscaping/Pool Service, Internet, Condo Fees	$
Auto	Car Loan/Lease, Gas, Insurance, Repairs, Parking, Bridge/Tolls	$
Insurance	Life, Disability, Long-Term Care, Liability (Umbrella Policy)	$
Food	Groceries, Eating Out	$
Personal Care	Clothing, Dry Cleaning, Cosmetics, Health Club Dues/Trainer, Entertainment, Country Club Dues, Association Memberships, Vacations, Hobbies, Education, Magazines, Gifts	$
Medical	Health Care Insurance, Dental Insurance, Prescription and Monthly Medicines, Chiropractic/Therapist, Doctor, or Dentist Expenses	$
Children	Child Support, Babysitter/Childcare, Tuition, Activities (sports, drama, art), Clothing, Tutoring, College Funding	$
Misc.	School Loans, Credit Card Expenses, Loan Payments, Anything Else	$
	Total Expenses	$
	Total Expenses with Murphy's Law Factor (add 10%)	$
	Total Income minus Total Expenses (incl. Murphy's Law Factor)	$
	TOTAL NET CASH FLOW Available for Savings (copy from line above)	$

When you've finished the exercise: Whew! That was a lot of work, pulling together files and paperwork from all sorts of places. But now, not only do you have a written statement of what you're spending each month, but you have a great reason to do something every Automatic Millionaire needs to do: GET ORGANIZED. If your financial records were scattered, use this opportunity to create a detailed filing system so you can always find what you need. To find a tool to help you do this, visit **www.finishrich.com** (and search the resource center for: "FinishRich File Folder System"). There you will find our free tool to get your financial papers at home organized in less than an hour.

"WE WATCHED OUR LATTE FACTOR."

After you add up your income and expense numbers, you might be thinking the same thing I was while I was talking to Jim and Sue. Paying yourself first is wonderful, but life is expensive. There are always bills to pay. So unless you can seriously increase your income (which most people can't do), how is it possible to save the kind of money they did?

I asked Jim and Sue that question, and they had a ready answer. They told me that one of their families' most valuable lessons was that while other people were splurging every day on small luxuries—"wasting big money on small things," Jim called it—you could be saving that money and over time it would add up to quite a bankroll. In Jim and Sue's case, the small things had been cigarettes.

"Our parents pointed out that if we stopped wasting money on cigarettes, we could probably save enough in two years to make a down payment on a home," Jim said. In my classes, I call this The Latte Factor.® Jim and Sue were living proof that it worked!

BRAINSTORMING BREAK

What daily spending could you stop and what could that money buy?

TWO HOMES, NO MORTGAGES, ZERO DEBT

"But how did you end up with two homes, both mortgage-free?" I asked.

The trick was that instead of making one monthly mortgage payment, Jim and Sue paid half their monthly payment once every two weeks. By the end of each year, they had made an extra full mortgage payment, and that allowed them to pay off their home in twenty-three years instead of thirty. As a bonus, they saved tens of thousands of dollars in interest payments. So they bought a second, nicer house to live in and, by making mortgage payments every two weeks on that house as well, paid it off by the time they were in their early fifties, with a nice stream of income from the first house to boot.

"WE PAY CASH OR WE DON'T BUY."

I was completely impressed, but nothing impressed me more than Jim and Sue's complete lack of debt. "Sue's mom and dad taught us never to buy on credit," Jim said. "No matter how big they are, you pay for your purchases with cash or you don't buy."

The McIntyres had never carried credit card debt throughout their entire marriage; if they used the cards, they paid the full balance the next month. Most of the time, they didn't use the cards at all. They had bought all their cars used and paid cash.

Jim and Sue were typical of American millionaires. They were frugal, but not cheap. They didn't drive his-and-hers Porsches. Jim drove a Ford and wore a Timex. For them, it was more important to "be rich" than to "look rich." They lived simply and enjoyed knowing they were financially independent. They left the expensive toys—and all the debt that buys them—to other people.

Are you more concerned with being rich or looking rich? It's OK if you like to look rich once in a while—everybody likes to show off. But in the long run, being an Automatic Millionaire is about being rich behind the scenes. That means choosing cash over flash, buying what you need without debt rather than an expensive luxury that comes complete with an 18% interest rate. If you can teach yourself to be rich and not worry about looking rich, you'll be heading for Automatic Millionaire country at top speed.

EXERCISE
The "Look Rich/Be Rich" Challenge

Think of this as a financial diagnostic chart. Do you suffer from chronic Look Rich disease? We're going to conduct an examination and find out.

How to use it: In the first column, list your 10 most expensive possessions. Next, write down whether you paid cash or credit for them (if cash, bravo!). Next, did you buy that item in part because it makes you look wealthy? If you did, check the box. Next, do the payments on that item strain your finances each month to the point where you can't save anything? Next, write down whether you'd be willing to make a change that would save you money. In the final column, write down what you could do regarding that possession that would help you be rich rather than look rich. It doesn't necessarily have to be getting rid of your possession; it could mean tapping cash reserves to pay off a credit balance.

THE "LOOK RICH/BE RICH" CHALLENGE					
List Your Top 10 Possessions	Method of Payment–Cash or Credit	Makes Me Look Rich?	Strains My Finances?	Willing to Change?	Action to "Be Rich"
1 Porsche Roadster	Credit (Leased)	X	Yes	Yes	Buy a Toyota
2					
3					
4					
5					
6					
7					
8					
9					
10					

When you've finished the exercise: When you look with a critical eye at the luxuries you spend money on, does it makes sense to worry more about looking rich than being rich? Do you know people who go out of their way to look rich? What does that say about them? What do you think of them? I'll bet you think less of them since meeting Jim and Sue McIntyre.

MAKE IT AUTOMATIC.
NO DISCIPLINE REQUIRED.

I sat back and thought. Everything about the McIntyres' plan seemed so simple. But there had to be a catch. "Everything you're talking about makes sense," I said. "Cutting wasteful spending, accelerating your mortgage payments, paying yourself first, buying only with cash. I teach exactly those things in my seminars. But you must have phenomenal willpower."

"But that's just the point," Sue said. "We don't have phenomenal willpower."

Jim chimed in. "Here's the thing. Let's say you know you should do something, but you're afraid you may be tempted to do something else. How can you make sure you do the right thing?"

I shrugged. Jim went on. "You arrange to have the thing you should do happen automatically," he said.

Of course! That was how Jim and Sue had avoided temptation and continued to save so consistently: They had automated every financial transaction. They'd had money automatically deducted from their paychecks and deposited into their retirement accounts. They'd had their biweekly mortgage payments automatically taken out of their checking account. They'd set up an automatic deduction to invest in mutual funds. They'd even automated their giving to charitable organizations. It all made perfect sense.

EXERCISE
The Automatic Millionaire Advantage

You're probably aware of things like automatic bill payment from your bank. But did you know there are free services that you can use to automate almost every aspect of your financial life? If you want to be like Jim and Sue—financially independent, debt-free, and excited about early retirement—start automating your finances *now*.

How to use it: Put a check next to each financial activity that you've automated, whether it's paying your utility bills online or an automatic deduction for your 401(k) account. In the last column, write down the status of the automated activities—that is, your car is 80% paid off, you're putting away $600 a month for retirement, and so on.

THE AUTOMATIC MILLIONAIRE ADVANTAGE		
Financial activity	Automated? ✓	What is your next step?
Mortgage payment		
Car payment		
Retirement account contribution		
Bill pay		
College fund contribution		
Charitable giving		
Mutual fund or stock investment		
Credit card payments		
Emergency fund		
Other		

When you've finished the exercise: If you've automated even one area of your finances, give yourself a huge pat on the back. That's more than most people. But our goal is to automate *all* your finances. We'll talk more about specifics later, but today, start looking at ways you can automate those areas you're still doing manually. Look what it's done for Jim and Sue!

"WE DECIDED TO BECOME AUTOMATIC MILLIONAIRES."

I glanced down at the McIntyres' financial statements. They had started small, but the numbers had really added up. "This is really remarkable," I said.

Sue shook her head. "That's where you're wrong," she told me. "It's not remarkable. If we can do it, anyone can do it." And she was right. After all, there was nothing special about the McIntyres, at least not on the surface.

- They had a very average household income.
- They hadn't inherited any money.
- They weren't self-employed.

What *was* special about Jim and Sue was that they had taken action. They had set up a system that literally made it impossible for them to fail. As long as their automatic deductions were in place, willpower wasn't an issue. The money just kept growing. They had made wealth inevitable. They weren't boring or living on the cheap. They were really enjoying life, even more so because they were free from worries about money.

BRAINSTORMING BREAK

How are you like Jim and Sue McIntyre? What could you do to be more like Jim and Sue when it comes to your money?

As we shook hands and Jim and Sue left my office, it hit me. Anyone *could* do what the McIntyres had done. As long as they knew the steps to take and could arrange for everything to happen automatically, anybody *could* become an Automatic Millionaire. *That was the secret to wealth:*

MAKE IT AUTOMATIC!

EXERCISE
The Automatic Millionaire Commitment

After reading Jim and Sue McIntyre's story, I hope you can appreciate that what makes them extraordinary is that they're *not* extraordinary. They are two typical, hardworking, middle-class people who have built a wonderful life for themselves and a beautiful legacy for their kids. The only thing unusual about them is their dedication to the principles of the Automatic Millionaire.

Remember what I said before about the difference between millionaires and the paycheck-to-paycheck crowd? Millionaires know what works and apply it. That's what the McIntyres did . . . and you can do exactly the same thing. All you need to do is make the commitment.

How to use it: Just fill in your name and sign the Commitment. If you like, make two copies for you and your partner. Then I suggest making big photocopies of the page and tacking the Commitment to your office wall, the fridge, wherever you'll see it. That way, you'll have a constant reminder about your commitment to your future.

THE AUTOMATIC MILLIONAIRE COMMITMENT

I, _____, hereby promise that I will

take all the necessary steps to put my Automatic Millionaire plan

into action as soon as possible. I will complete this workbook, follow

the steps contained within, and guarantee myself, my partner, and my

family a future of financial security and personal fulfillment.

Signed, _____

Date _____

When you've finished the exercise: Bravo! You've just made a commitment that will change your life.

BECOMING RICH WAS NEVER SIMPLER

Jim and Sue McIntyre lived what I'm going to share with you in this workbook. They are proof that the secret to being wealthy and living the life you want has nothing to do with fancy Wall Street gimmicks or complicated financial formulas. Like all great ideas, it's very simple. That's why virtually anyone can do it!

As Jim and Sue left my office that day, I realized that I had to follow the same plan they did. Today, my wife and I are Automatic Millionaires, and so are many of our friends. This strategy works. In fact, once you have everything in place so there's no discipline required, it can't *not* work!

Later on, we're going to talk in greater detail about each of the key parts of the McIntyres' Automatic Millionaire plan: watching your Latte Factor, Paying Yourself First, Making It Automatic, and so on. But right now, just say to yourself, "I can do this. I can become an Automatic Millionaire. It can start today." That's no exaggeration. It really can.

KEY POINTS TO REMEMBER FROM THIS CHAPTER

- It's more important to be rich than to look rich.
- Set your retirement goals today.
- Your plan must be automatic to succeed.
- You don't need to increase your income to be rich, just increase what you save.

EXERCISE
The Automatic Millionaire Motivator

At the end of each chapter is a Motivator. Fill it out before you turn the page, while the information is fresh in your mind. You'll capture the excitement you feel and turn that into action steps you can take today and in the coming days to make your Automatic Millionaire plan a reality!

How to use it: First, record the ways in which your eyes were opened by what you read about the McIntyres. Next, jot down a to-do list of action steps for the next day and the next week. Finally, because this information can benefit everyone, list a few friends or family members to share your Automatic Millionaire insights with. Who knows, maybe you and all your friends can retire early, too!

THE AUTOMATIC MILLIONAIRE MOTIVATOR

What is your biggest breakthrough from this chapter?

1

2

3

What are the most important actions you want to take in the next 24 hours?

1

2

3

What are the most important actions you want to take in the next 7 days?

1

2

3

What from this chapter do you want to share with someone else in your life?	Why?
1	
2	
3	

When you've finished the exercise: Pick the top action item from each list and get going on it *today*. You'll find yourself completely energized when you take positive action!

Now you've met the McIntyres, my inspiration for *The Automatic Millionaire*. You've seen what they did to achieve complete financial freedom and peace of mind. Most of all, you've seen that anyone can do it. To me, that's the most thrilling thing about *The Automatic Millionaire*: Anyone can become one!

Let's move ahead and take a look at the best and most overlooked way to save money: knowing your Latte Factor.

CHAPTER TWO

THE LATTE FACTOR®:

Becoming an Automatic Millionaire on Just a Few Dollars a Day

IT'S NOT WHAT WE MAKE, IT'S WHAT WE SPEND

Most people believe that the secret to becoming rich is increasing their income. But ask anyone you know who got a raise recently if they've saved more money, and they'll probably say no. Why? Because generally, **the more we make, the more we spend.**

Becoming a millionaire over your working life is *not* about working more hours and making more money. I said this last chapter, and it bears repeating:

> *You probably earn enough already to be a millionaire by the time you retire.*

Look at Jim and Sue McIntyre, who averaged only $35,000 a year income during their lifetime. If you take only one thing away from their story, it should be that how much you earn has almost no bearing on whether or not you will build wealth.

IF SPENDING IS THE DISEASE, SAVING IS THE CURE

Spending is an epidemic in our society. Do you have any of the symptoms?

- You're working harder but never seem to have enough money.
- You've already planned how you'll spend your money before you get it.
- There's never anything to save at the end of the month.
- You have no idea where your money goes.

We live in a consumer culture. Our society tells us that it's not just OK to spend everything we earn on things we don't need. It's good. It builds the economy. It's *patriotic* to go shopping. But there's a big problem with this: If you're spending everything you make, living paycheck to paycheck, you're on a treadmill, running a race you can't ever win. It looks like this:

GO TO WORK.

MAKE MONEY.

SPEND MONEY.

GO TO WORK.

MAKE MONEY.

SPEND MONEY.

GO TO WORK.

We call it the "rat race," but I think maybe those little rats have more sense than some people. Rats do just what they need to survive and no more. But some people work long hours for decades only to wind up with little savings and a mountain of debt. Why? Because no matter how much they make, at the end of the month their paycheck is already spent.

It's a vicious cycle, one you don't want to fall into. If you're in it, you want to get out of it *now*. And you can.

AN AUTOMATIC MILLIONAIRE SUCCESS STORY

I just finished reading *The Automatic Millionaire* . . . my Latte Factor has always been spending money on dinner and drinks with friends. A typical Friday night out in the D.C. area can cost anywhere from $60 to $100 per person.

I complained to my wife one day that I hadn't been able to save much in my regular checking, so we looked at my bank statements and realized that our occasional night out was costing me much more than it was costing her. Naturally, I asked for her consultation.

Using [your] strategy, I have been able to save $20–$50 a month from my entertainment budget. My wife and I plan our menu for the week and make it a point to incorporate interesting dishes into our weekly bill of fare. Then we shop for the ingredients and cook together on two or three of the weekday evenings. We've experimented with Thai, Moroccan, Armenian, Cajun, and Indian dishes in our first year together.

By cutting down on what I spend on entertainment and lunch, I've been able to contribute the maximum amount to my Roth IRA and 14% of my income to my Thrift Savings Plan.

Zachariah Brevis
Alexandria, VA

IS YOUR INCOME MAKING YOU LESS FREE?

Wealth is about the freedom to live a life that's in tune with your values. When you're not worried about money, you're free, free to enjoy life to its fullest. You're probably making more than you were ten years ago. Has your increase in earning power made you more free? Or are you just deeper in debt?

By the time you're finished with *The Automatic Millionaire Workbook*, you'll know how to use the power of your earnings to create the freedom you crave. And you're going to start by learning your Latte Factor.

BRAINSTORMING BREAK

How free does your income make you? Are you as free as you should be?

WHAT IS THE LATTE FACTOR®?

As Jim and Sue McIntyre discovered, most of us waste a lot of our money on "small things." When we spend money on "small things" every day, that money adds up to a big amount. We don't realize that if we saved that money, it would quickly add up to life-changing piles of cash.

When we're looking at ways to cut spending, we usually look at big-ticket items. But really, we should be looking at the little amounts we throw away every day without thinking about it on things ranging from lattes at Starbucks to a pack of cigarettes. If, instead of spending money on small daily expenses that drain away our cash, we invested even part of that money, we'd be building some pretty significant wealth.

I call those small, unexamined daily expenses "The Latte Factor." The McIntyres understood its power. Remember, they quit buying cigarettes and in two years had saved enough for a down payment on a home! You're going to gain the same awareness of what you're spending on "small things," and you're going to learn how to redirect that wasted cash to help you build your fortune. It doesn't matter what the numbers on your paycheck are. By knowing your Latte Factor, you can start to build real wealth and finally do what the rich do: ***make your money work for you, instead of the other way around.***

SAVING MONEY EVERY DAY . . .
IMPOSSIBLE?

The Latte Factor has become an international metaphor for how we fritter away would-be fortunes every day on small purchases. But it's based on an actual discussion I had during a four-week investment course I was teaching. A young woman named Kim said, "David, your ideas are good in theory, but they don't have anything to do with reality."

I was intrigued. "What do you mean?" I said.

Kim replied, "You make this idea of saving money seem easy, but in reality it's impossible. You talk about saving $5 or $10 a day like it's no big deal. Well, for me, it is a big deal. In fact, it's impossible. I'm living paycheck to paycheck. So how can I possibly save $5 to $10 a day? It's just not realistic."

Everybody else was nodding. I realized it was time to toss my lesson plan and address Kim's concern. I said, "Kim, since others in this room obviously feel the same way you do, let's really look at what you're saying." I went to the blackboard. "Let's go through your expenses for a typical day."

AN AUTOMATIC MILLIONAIRE SUCCESS STORY

I just wanted to take a moment to say thank you for *The Automatic Millionaire* and for inspiring me. I increased my 401(k) from 6% to 10% with plans to increase it 2% with every salary increase that I receive. I've opened an IRA, increased the money I'm saving in my Security Basket and have opened funds for my Dream Basket, which will go towards the purchase of my first home. At 33, I feel that I am ready to move full steam ahead without worrying about my financial future. After all, why worry? It's all automatic and I will retire early as a millionaire. Thank you so much for inspiring me and giving me something to share with others.

Denise Grant
Brooklyn, NY

"MY LATTES ARE COSTING ME *WHAT*?"

So we did exactly that. Kim took me through every step of a typical day—and all the "must-have" purchases that she made as a part of that day. As the class went on, I kept a running tally on the chalkboard, and this is what we found out:

- Every day, Kim stopped at Starbucks for a double nonfat latte and a muffin. Total cost: $5.00.
- Most days, she took a break at 10 A.M. and went with some friends to get a blended juice drink with ginkgo biloba added, along with a PowerBar to boost her blood sugar. Total cost: $7.20.

I stopped there. "So, Kim," I said, "we're not even at lunch and you've spent more than $10. And you haven't really had anything to eat yet!" That broke up the whole class. But my message was serious. So I went on.

"Kim, we all spend small amounts of money every day without thinking, money that would add up to a huge amount if we saved it. Let me show you something I think will amaze you."

I pulled out my calculator and input some numbers. If Kim, age 23, saved just $5 a day and put it into her retirement plan, she would save $150 a month, almost $2,000 a year. At a 10% annual return (what the stock market has averaged over the last 50 years) . . . I asked Kim how much she thought she would have by the time she was 65.

She shrugged. "Maybe a hundred thousand?" I shook my head. "Two hundred thousand?" she said.

"Try again," I said. Her eyes began to get wide. "Five hundred thousand?"

"How about nearly $1.2 million?"

Kim's jaw hit the floor. "Actually, don't you work for a company that matches employee 401(k) contributions?" I asked. She nodded. "Well, if your company matched just 50% of what you put in, you'd be investing nearly $3,000 a year, and by age 65 that would add up to . . ." I punched a few more buttons, and voilà! "Roughly $1,742,000."

I could see the lightbulb go on over Kim's head. "David," she said, "are you trying to tell me that *my lattes are costing me nearly $2 million!?*" In unison, everyone in the room cried, "YES!"

The Latte Factor was born.

EXERCISE
The Latte Factor Numbers Game

I'd like you to do the same thing Kim did: mentally walk through your typical day and take your best guess about how you spend your money. You don't have to be exact; I'm going to have you do that later. But by "guesstimating" how much you spend every day on little purchases, you'll start to get an idea of just what The Latte Factor can mean.

How to use it: Go through a typical workday and write down what you usually buy, from a morning newspaper to a cup of java. At the end, add up what you usually spend. Then go to the right column and start multiplying to see how that money adds up. It adds up fast!

THE LATTE FACTOR NUMBERS GAME			
1 How Much You Spend in a Day		**2** How Much Could You Save...	
What You Buy	**Cost**		
Smoothie	$3.75	in a week? (day × 7) $ _____	
_____	_____	in a month? (week × 4) $ _____	
_____	_____	in a year? (month × 12) $ _____	
_____	_____	in a decade? (year × 10) $ _____	
What you spend in a typical day:	$ _____	in 20 years? (decade × 2) $ _____	

When you've finished the exercise: Were you surprised by how much you spend on an average day and how fast it adds up? Don't be. Most of us have a Latte Factor. But what you've just done is become aware of it, and that's the first step toward making that money work for you.

SMALL AMOUNTS + TIME = A BIG DIFFERENCE

Most of us have a daily spending habit that we don't think about, but which wastes substantial amounts of money. If we just changed our habits a little, we could change our destiny. And let's say you're only earning 6% per year. You'd still end up with hundreds of thousands of dollars. In Kim's case, earning 6% would give her $559,523 at age 65—still a lot of money.

What makes The Latte Factor so powerful is this:

Small amounts of money make a big difference when you save them every day and apply the miracle of compound interest.

THE TRUTH IS IN THE NUMBERS

The impact of The Latte Factor on people is really incredible. After all the complicated advice they've been hearing about how to create wealth, they can't believe that something this simple can create so much future wealth for them. But it can. For instance:

IF YOU QUIT BUYING A LATTE A DAY, YOU'D SAVE ...	
Every day	$3.50
Every month	$105
In a year	$1,260
In a decade	$12,600

And lattes are just the beginning. What if you're a pack-a-day smoker? In most big cities, cigarettes are so heavily taxed that a pack runs from five to seven dollars. So you've got both a financial risk and a health risk. Let's average it out at six bucks and see what you'd save by quitting:

IF YOU QUIT SMOKING, YOU'D SAVE ...	
Every day	$7
Every month	$210
In a year	$2,520
In a decade	$25,200

Twenty-five thousand dollars! That's a lot of money after just 10 years. Invest just that money by itself at 10% and in another 20 years you'd have over $183,000. Plus you'd be more likely to be around to enjoy your wealth.

> ### AN AUTOMATIC MILLIONAIRE SUCCESS STORY
>
> Well, I'm already on the last chapter of *The Automatic Millionaire* and just now writing to you about my own Latte Factor. It's your own fault since your book just makes me want to keep reading and learning about how to become an Automatic Millionaire. Anyway, between my daily coffee and drinks, my Latte Factor for one day is $9.10 and in 40 years at a 10 percent return it would be worth $1,726,474!!
>
> Well that made me a little mad at first (mostly at myself and some at the coffee for tasting so good) and I decided to use that money for my future. I started reading your book on Monday, and by Friday I have already set up a Roth IRA with automatic biweekly payments at my local bank, am researching for my Rainy Day accounts, and know how much house I can afford using the biweekly mortgage payment plan! I did all this while working 14-hour duty days, but it's definitely worth it.
>
> I only buy items with cash and don't own a credit card (to the shock and dismay of my friends). Now your book is completely changing my mind about actually having a plan to retire rich. Thanks.
>
> **Blair Mahoney**
> **Perkasie, PA**

USE THE POWER OF THE LATTE FACTOR

Whether it's lattes, cigarettes, candy bars, or cab fare when you could walk, daily spending adds up to big money. And it adds up faster when there are two of you. Let's say you're in a relationship. You and your spouse figure out you each spend $20 a day on frivolous purchases, from morning juices to newspapers. You agree to each cut spending by $10 per day and invest that money in a retirement account. How much could you save by saving $20 a day together?

IF YOU SAVED $20 PER DAY ($600 A MONTH) AND INVESTED IT AT A 10% ANNUAL RETURN, YOU'D HAVE . . .

1 year	$7,539
2 years	$15,868
5 years	$46,462
10 years	$122,907
20 years	$455,621
30 years	$1,356,293
40 years	$3,794,448

Could you find a way to save $20 a day if you knew you could turn that money into nearly half a million bucks in 20 years?

USE THE LATTE FACTOR CALCULATOR

If you want to do some of your own calculations and see what incredible results decades of compound interest can produce, just go to **www.finishrich.com.** Click on "Resources," then on "Calculators," and use the Latte Factor Calculator to figure out just how rich finding your Latte Factor could make you. While you're at it, read the Latte Factor success stories—of real people just like you who have used this simple idea to change their financial future.

KICK YOURSELF IN THE "YEAH, BUT . . ."

And now, here come the "yeah, buts." That's what people do to rationalize their current situation. "Yeah, butters" work hard to find ways to improve their financial condition, only to "yeah, but" their way right past the answers.

Are you a "yeah, butter"? You are if you're saying things like this to yourself:

"Yeah, but I'll never be able to earn a 10% return on my money." Wrong. Later on, I'll show you how you can earn exactly that over time.

"Yeah, but with inflation, a million dollars won't be worth much in 30 years." Wrong. It will be worth more than you think. Remember, your earnings will increase to meet inflation, so you can save more. Plus, a million bucks will be worth a lot more than the nothing you'll have if you don't save.

Sound familiar? If your first reaction to The Latte Factor was "Yeah, but . . . ," it's time to nip that in the bud with this exercise.

EXERCISE
The "Yeah, But" Debunker

"Yeah, but" is the sound of poverty, debt, and a life of working hard to get nowhere. So you're going to confront your "Yeah, buts" and learn why they're nothing but hot air.

How to use it: On the left, write down the "yeah, but" reasons you've been thinking about when it comes to saving money by knowing your Latte Factor. Then, on the right, look at your excuse with a critical eye and write down what you could do to overcome that excuse.

THE "YEAH, BUT" DEBUNKER	
"Yeah, But" Excuse	**The Reality**
I only make $30,000 a year.	*I could bring my lunch and save $25 a week.*

When you've finished the exercise: Good work. It's not easy to confront your own fears and excuses. But by doing it, you've cleared one of the major obstacles to becoming an Automatic Millionaire out of your way. Now you're ready to discover your own Latte Factor and change how you spend money forever!

FIND YOUR PERSONAL LATTE FACTOR

To put the power of The Latte Factor to work for you, you need to know what your own Latte Factor is. The sooner you find that out, the sooner you can eliminate it and start putting that money aside.

You could guess the ways you're spending your money each day, but I don't recommend it. Latte Factor spending is habitual; you might not even realize what your daily spending is costing you. So I've given you a tool to find out.

In *The Automatic Millionaire*, I had you fill out a one-day Latte Factor form. But here we need more information, so we're going to ask you to work a little harder and complete The Latte Factor Seven-Day Challenge.

EXERCISE
The Latte Factor Seven-Day Challenge

How to use it: Make photocopies of the Challenge page or download the forms at **www.finishrich.com.** Then just follow the steps:

1. Take a fresh copy of the form with you every day for seven days.
2. Write down every penny you spend from the time you walk out of the house in the morning to the time you go to bed at night. That means:
    - Things you pay cash for
    - Things you write a check for
    - Things you use a debit card for
    - Things you buy with a credit card
    - Tolls
    - Tips
    - Money for parking meters
3. At the end of each day, calculate your Latte Factor results.

THE LATTE FACTOR SEVEN-DAY CHALLENGE

Day of the Week _____   Date _____

What I Bought	What I Spent	Wasted Money? "✓" for Yes

Today's Latte Factor Total (cost of checked items): $ _____

When you've tracked your Latte Factor for seven days, you're ready to "do the math" and discover how changing your Latte Factor spending could really change your life:

EXERCISE
The Latte Factor Math

How to use it: Figure your average daily Latte Factor. Then multiply it to learn how much you could save in a month, a year, and 10 years. Again, go to **www.finishrich.com,** then click on "Resources," then "Calculators," and then "Latte Factor Calculator." Use the calculator to figure out what that money could turn into. The amount will amaze you and open your eyes to the possibilities.

THE LATTE FACTOR MATH

My total Latte Factor spending for the week:	$_____
My average daily Latte Factor (total ÷ 7):	$_____
My Latte Factor for one month (average × 30):	$_____
My Latte Factor for one year (average × 365):	$_____
My Latte Factor for ten years (average × 3,650):	$_____

If I invested my Latte Factor for . . .
(using the calculator at www.finishrich.com)

1 year at 10%, it would be worth:	$_____
5 years at 10%, it would be worth:	$_____
10 years at 10%, it would be worth:	$_____
20 years at 10%, it would be worth:	$_____
30 years at 10%, it would be worth:	$_____
40 years at 10%, it would be worth:	$_____

When you've finished the exercise: Give yourself a big hand! If you've made it through all seven days of the Challenge, you've just learned more about becoming wealthy in a week than most folks learn in a lifetime. You've learned that you *do* have money to save and that there's no such thing as an insignificant amount of money. Now you're ready to move on with your Automatic Millionaire plan!

AN AUTOMATIC MILLIONAIRE SUCCESS STORY

I'm reading *The Automatic Millionaire* right now, and I'm astonished! I'd heard about spending big money on the little things, but until you laid it out like this, I never realized how much money I've been wasting. Take today, for example:

I was running late to work, so had no time for breakfast at home (something that happens at least three times a week). I bought a bagel w/cream cheese, coffee, and water bottle for the day. Total for breakfast: $5.65.

For the same reason as above, I bought the lunch "special" at work, which included a drink. Total for lunch: $7.50.

Now I'm sitting here eating it, and imagining if I'd brown-bagged it. I would have saved over $13 SO FAR TODAY!!! That's at least $10 that I could have put into a retirement plan. Waking up a few minutes earlier in the morning is definitely worth a million dollars down the road.

Nancy Ocampo
Los Angeles, CA

DID YOU REALIZE HOW MUCH
YOU WERE SPENDING?

It's stunning (or maybe appalling) to see how much you really spend—and what you spend it on—in a typical day, written out in black-and-white figures that are impossible to deny. There's something about it that can motivate you to make real changes in the way you spend.

So what is your Latte Factor? Before, I used lattes and cigarettes as examples, but it could be anything you spend money on: the Microbrew Factor, the Gum Factor, the Eating Out Factor, the Emergency Lip Balm Factor, and so on. What's your factor called?

NAME YOUR OWN FACTOR

What do you spend money on each day that could be costing you a fortune?

My _____ Factor

IF YOU WANT TO GET RICH, LEARN YOUR LATTE FACTOR

Congratulations on reading this far. At this point, I hope you're excited by what you've learned. I hope you've had your eyes opened to the revelation that no matter how much money you make, you can be rich by taking control of your Latte Factor.

Now you're ready to discover your Latte Factor and start saving money you didn't even know you had! It's time to take what you've learned and move on to some immediate, powerful action. Remember, inspiration unused is entertainment.

KEY POINTS TO REMEMBER FROM THIS CHAPTER

- Money is about freedom.
- We all have mindless daily spending habits called The Latte Factor.
- That money, saved instead of spent, adds up fast.
- You won't know your Latte Factor unless you deliberately track it.

EXERCISE
The Latte Factor Motivator

How to use it: First, record the ways your eyes were opened by learning about The Latte Factor. Next, jot down a to-do list of action steps for the next 24 hours and the next 7 days. Finally, list a few people with whom you want to share your Latte Factor insights.

THE LATTE FACTOR MOTIVATOR

What is your biggest breakthrough from this chapter?

1

2

3

What are the most important actions you want to take in the next 24 hours?

1

2

3

What are the most important actions you want to take in the next 7 days?

1

2

3

What from this chapter do you want to share with someone else in your life?	Why?
1	
2	
3	

When you've finished the exercise: Again, don't wait too long to act. Take some actions today, before you turn to the next chapter. You'll feel fantastic when you do!

You've discovered one of the great, untold secrets of wealth in this country—and what's more, you've learned how to use it. Now we're going to move on to the idea that will save you from EVER having to write a budget again and will set your Automatic Millionaire plan in motion. . . .

CHAPTER THREE

LEARN TO PAY YOURSELF FIRST

Let's talk about budgets. You're never going to need one again.

Wait a minute. Wasn't the point of The Latte Factor to track how much you're spending so you can cut back and save? And doesn't saving mean being on a budget?

No. The point of The Latte Factor was to demonstrate that you earn enough, right now, to start saving and investing and building future wealth. And that means throwing away your budget.

BUDGETS JUST DON'T WORK

Why do most people think they need a budget? Because that's what their parents or grandparents told them. Maybe a financial expert. But were they rich? Were they free from financial worries?

Budgets don't work because they're hard. Just like diets, budgets ask you to deprive yourself today for a reward tomorrow. We're not good at that sort of thing. It goes against human nature.

Budgets don't work because they ask you to be disciplined and be controlled. But we don't like being controlled; we want to be *in* control. And for most of us, we're too busy to be disciplined—it takes too much time. You should never let your money control you. You should be able to do this with very little discipline and time commitment. So, for your own good, please dump those budgets in the garbage. There really is an easier way. I'm going to give you an alternative—a system that allows you to tear up your budget and never worry about it again.

EXERCISE
No More Budgeting!

Living on a budget is so ingrained that it's hard for many people to imagine not living on one. So in case you're having a rough time with the idea, we're going to map out, in black and white, just how good you are (or aren't) at staying within your budget and saving money. Trust me, this will be an eye-opener.

How to use it: At the top, write down the month you're using as an example (ideally, last month). In the first column, you'll find boxes listing typical monthly expenses, with a Miscellaneous box for others I didn't think of. In column two, write down what you budgeted for each expense last month. If you're not sure, take your best guess. In column three, write down what you actually spent last month for each expense. And in the last column, write down how much you were under or over budget for each.

Once that's done, add the totals for columns two and three. If two's total is higher than three's, congratulations. You lived within your budget, something most people don't do. If column three is higher than column two, you're over budget. Below that, write down how much you were over or under budget for all expenses for the month. Then look at the same month and write down how much you were able to save in a retirement account. Did you save anything?

If you want a broader picture, I suggest you do this exercise for two or three months. I'll bet you start to see a pattern. When you're finished, go to the last box and write down any reasons you can think of why you should continue budgeting. Are there any that make sense for you?

NO MORE BUDGETING!

Month _____

1. Expenses	2. What You Budgeted Last Month	3. What You Spent Last Month	4. How Much Over or Under Budget
Example: Food	*$300*	*$450*	*$150 over*
Food			
Utilities			
Clothing			
Entertainment			
Car			
Misc.			
Total:	$ _____	$ _____	$ _____

Amount Over/Under Budget for the Month: $ _____

Amount Saved Toward Retirement Last Month: $ _____

List 3 reasons you should continue budgeting (if you can):

1.

2.

3.

When you've finished the exercise: You may feel like tossing your latest budget into the garbage can. Good! Do it! Budgets are the last thing you need if you're going to become an Automatic Millionaire. What you need is what I'm going to share with you next.

IF THIS WERE THE ONLY THING YOU DID, YOU'D BE RICH

If you want to be rich, all you have to do is make the decision to do something most people don't do:

Pay Yourself First.

What does that mean? When most people bring home their paycheck, the first thing they do is pay everyone else: the landlord, the credit card company, the government. If there's anything "left over" at the end, they pay themselves by saving.

That is completely, positively, financially *backward*. If you pay everyone else first, you will *never* get rich. Think about it this way: There are six primary ways to get rich in this country:

1. Win it.
2. Marry it.
3. Inherit it.
4. Sue for it.
5. Budget for it.
6. **Pay Yourself First.**

EXERCISE
The "What Are the Odds" Get-Rich Lottery

Let's have a little fun with the great American get-rich-quick schemes. I'm always amazed at how many people believe that getting rich "just happens"
somehow. It doesn't. But you can plan to get rich by becoming an Automatic
Millionaire. To see how silly, petty, or downright ridiculous the other meth-
ods really are, and how Paying Yourself First is the only true, dependable
way to build genuine long-term wealth, try this exercise.

How to use it: Just read the six scenarios for getting rich and what you'd
have to do to make each one happen. Then rate your odds, from "Dream On,"
or no chance in this life, to "Certain," which means you can practically guarantee success. At the bottom, write down the method that gives you the best
odds of building real wealth.

THE "WHAT ARE THE ODDS" GET-RICH LOTTERY		
The Method	**What You'd Need to Do**	**Your Chances of Success**
Win It	Have the one winning lottery ticket out of 20 or 30 million sold each month.	Dream On | | | | | | | | | Certain
Marry It	Find someone wealthy who's not married and whom you could live with for 30–40 years.	Dream On | | | | | | | | | Certain
Inherit It	Be lucky enough to have a rich relative and mean enough to wait around for them to die.	Dream On | | | | | | | | | Certain
Sue for It	Spend years in court with no guarantees, only to pay 40% to your lawyer.	Dream On | | | | | | | | | Certain
Budget for It	Brown-bag it, watch every penny, and never have a major emergency expense.	Dream On | | | | | | | | | Certain
Pay Yourself First	Put 10% of every paycheck into a retirement account.	Dream On | | | | | | | | | Certain

Which method for getting rich makes the most sense for you?

When you've finished the exercise: Now you have some valuable perspective on the sillier ideas people have about hitting pay dirt. For instance, did you know that you literally have a better chance of being hit by lightning than of winning most state lotteries? But the odds of getting rich by Paying Yourself First are excellent . . . if you take action today!

BRAINSTORMING BREAK

What plans have you had for getting rich?

WHAT DOES "PAY YOURSELF FIRST" MEAN?

So it's clear that Pay Yourself First is the one get-rich plan that actually makes sense. But what does it mean? Look at it this way: When you earn a dollar, before that money even gets into your paycheck, Uncle Sam gets his cut for federal income tax. Then the state takes its five cents. On top of that, you have Social Security taxes, Medicaid, and unemployment taxes. That's 35 to 40 cents out of your hard-earned dollar.

It wasn't always this way. Before 1943, people took home everything they earned and the government came calling for taxes in spring. But people often didn't save enough money to pay their taxes. The government's solution to this problem was brilliant: The IRS *automated the process*, taking the money out of people's paychecks before the checks even reached the workers. The government set up a system to Pay Itself First.

That's *exactly* what you're going to do. You're going to set up a system that ensures that you get paid automatically—even before the IRS does. How sweet is that?

AN AUTOMATIC MILLIONAIRE SUCCESS STORY

Since reading *The Automatic Millionaire*, I have increased my 401(k) to 10% and I'm working on writing down everything I spend. I was also able to start putting $25 a week into an automatic savings account. The next step is to set up a biweekly mortgage payment plan. I'm now paying myself first because if I can pay the government, I can pay myself. Thanks for the inspiration.

Joyce Franklin
Lynchburg, VA

WHOM ARE YOU REALLY WORKING FOR?

Driving down the freeway not long ago, I saw a billboard that read, "Who you work for is waiting for you at home." First it made me laugh, then it made me think.

Our employers want us to think we're working for them. The government wants us to think we're working for a healthy economy. But we're really working for ourselves. The reason you go to work is to provide for and protect yourself and those you love. *You* are your first priority.

But if that's true, why aren't more people creating financial plans centered on themselves? Before you start laying out a financial plan, you've got to ask a crucial question: "Am I really working for myself?"

EXERCISE
How Many Hours Did You Work for Yourself?

This exercise will give you more perspective on your working life than any other. You'll understand, maybe for the first time, how much of your workday you've devoted to your own needs . . . and you'll be determined to spend more of your work time working for yourself.

How to use it: Fill in each box and do the math.

HOW MANY HOURS DID YOU WORK FOR YOURSELF?
a. Last week, I worked a total of _____ hours.
b. I earn $_____ an hour before taxes.
c. Last week, I put aside $_____ for my retirement.
d. So last week, I worked _____ hours for myself (c ÷ b).

When you've finished the exercise: Now you know what you're doing today. Tomorrow, you can start working *more* for yourself.

IT'S ABOUT HOW MUCH MONEY YOU SAVE

Working for yourself is about saving money toward your future. How much should you be working for yourself? Let's consider someone who earns $50,000 a year before taxes:

- That person earns roughly $1,000 a week (with two weeks off for vacation)
- That's roughly $25 an hour for a 40-hour week

A good benchmark for retirement savings is between 10% and 15% of your income. Let's split the difference and say 12.5%. Now, 12.5% of $1,000 is $125. So if you're earning $1,000 a week, you should be saving $125 a week, or $25 a day. In other words, you should be working at least one hour per day for yourself.

Unfortunately, most people don't. According to the U.S. Department of Commerce, the average American works barely 22 minutes a day for himself, and saves below 5% of what he earns. One out of five workers saves nothing.

AN AUTOMATIC MILLIONAIRE SUCCESS STORY

We're feeling great today after reading *The Automatic Millionaire*. Despite having three special-needs kids and the mounting bills that accompany them, we started the automatic deduction process 10 years ago with my husband's 401(k). You really do not miss what you cannot see! That automatic deduction has grown from zero to over $126,000 even though we have had to tweak our percentage to match our financial needs. Despite dropping to 2% some years, we are back to 18%.... Like you said, the only true way to do this is through automation.

We live comfortably below our means, knowing our future will be set! We also make one extra payment a year on our mortgage. Not bad for a family beset with many challenges.

Marie Louise Kier
Chester Springs, PA

STARTING TODAY, YOU'RE WORKING FOR *YOU*

That's tragic. Why would you work hard for decades and NOT work at least one hour a day for yourself?

You shouldn't. An hour a day is really not a lot to ask in return for a bright future. You deserve at least that.

LET'S GET BUSY!

Here's the plan you've been waiting for. Starting today, you should:

1. Decide to Pay Yourself First.
2. Work at least one hour per day for yourself.

3. Open a retirement account if you don't already have one.
4. Fund it with 10% (an hour a day) of your gross income.
5. **Make it automatic.**

That's it. If you follow just those basic steps, you will be rich by the time you retire. I'll explain how to do each one of these things as we move through *The Automatic Millionaire Workbook*.

PAY YOURSELF BEFORE YOU PAY THE GOVERNMENT

Congratulations on deciding to Pay Yourself First at least one hour's pay per day. But don't just put that money into your savings account. The key to Paying Yourself First is to pay yourself before you pay the government, using a pretax retirement account. With a 401(k), 403(b), IRA, or SEP IRA, you can keep everything you earn without the government taxing one cent of it.

There is no catch! Starting tomorrow, you simply arrange to have 10% of your gross income automatically deducted from your paycheck and deposited in a pretax retirement account. If you did only that, you would eventually accumulate more wealth than 90% of the population.

AN AUTOMATIC MILLIONAIRE SUCCESS STORY

After reading *The Automatic Millionaire*, my first financial goal was to become debt-free within a year. So 20% of our family income went toward paying off our debt. It was limiting our available money but it was no burden to us since we had decided to simplify our lives by cutting down on shopping, doing more meaningful activities, and driving our paid-off cars longer instead of getting a newer one on consumer loan. At the same time, I unexpectedly had the opportunity to do some freelance work in addition to my regular job. Now, after only one year we paid off all of our debt ($12,000) plus I was able to establish a 4-month financial cushion for security. Before I read your book, I would have spent the extra money pretty quickly for all kinds of reasons but I was determined that this time, I would act differently. This time I had goals. It was not as hard as I expected it to be. For the first time, our family will not have to live paycheck to paycheck. I can't wait to achieve the next goals on my list and to put more of your advice to work. Once again, thank you very much!

Brigitte Rush
Seattle, WA

WHY THIS WON'T HURT A BIT

When I tell people about the Pay Yourself First system, the first objection is "There's no way I could save an hour's pay every day!" That's a perfectly normal reaction. The idea of cutting your take-home pay by, say, $200 every two weeks, or $14 a day, might seem scary. But as we saw when we looked at your Latte Factor, and as you'll see in the next chapter, it's actually easier to save that money than you might think.

As it turns out, automatically deducting $14 a day from your pay actually reduces your *spendable* income by only $10 a day. The next exercise will explain in detail how this is possible, but basically it works this way: When you move money from your paycheck into a pretax retirement account, you don't pay income tax on that money. So your paycheck goes down less than your retirement account goes up.

Still unclear? This exercise should do the trick.

EXERCISE
How Little Will It Hurt Today to Save for Tomorrow?

Thanks to the wonders of tax-deferred retirement accounts that Pay You First, investing 10% of your gross income will hit you in the wallet a lot less than you think. Use this worksheet to figure out how much saving 10% will cost you in spendable income each month.

How to use it: First, take a look at the example exercise. Then go step by step and fill in each box. You may want to grab your pocket calculator to make things easier and faster.

	HOW LITTLE WILL IT HURT TODAY TO SAVE FOR TOMORROW?	
	Today—Example	
a.	My gross annual income	**$50,000**
b.	My tax rate	**25%**
c.	How much I'm taxed on my salary (a × b)	**$12,500**
d.	What I actually take home each year (a − c)	**$37,500**
	Tomorrow—Example	
e.	10% of my gross income (my pretax savings goal)	**$5,000**
f.	My gross income minus my pretax savings goal (my new taxable income) (a − e)	**$45,000**
g.	How much tax I'll pay on my new taxable income (f × 25%)	**$11,250**
h.	My new annual take-home income (f − g)	**$33,750**
i.	How much less I'm really taking home per year (d − h)	**$3,750**
j.	How much less per month (i ÷ 12)	**$312.50**
k.	How much less per day (j ÷ 30)	**$10.42**

Conclusion:

Saving $5,000 per year for my retirement will cost me $3,750, or $10.42 per day.

	HOW LITTLE WILL IT HURT TODAY TO SAVE FOR TOMORROW?	
	Today	
a.	My gross annual income	$_____
b.	My tax rate	_____%
c.	How much I'm taxed on my salary (a × b)	$_____
d.	What I actually take home each year (a − c)	$_____
	Tomorrow	
e.	10% of my gross income (my pretax savings goal)	$_____
f.	My gross income minus my pretax savings goal (my new taxable income) (a − e)	$_____
g.	How much tax I'll pay on my new taxable income (f × 25%)	$_____
h.	My new annual take-home income (f − g)	$_____
i.	How much less I'm really taking home per year (d − h)	$_____
j.	How much less per month (i ÷ 12)	$_____
k.	How much less per day (j ÷ 30)	$_____

Conclusion:

Saving $_____ per year for my retirement will cost me $_____ , or $_____ per day.

When you've finished the exercise: What a revelation, right? Pretax accounts mean that saving will affect your take-home pay much less than you'd think. If you're making a decent average income, I'll bet you can save that 10% of your income for the cost of your Latte Factor.

THE "PAY YOURSELF FIRST" FORMULA

Now you know that you can save enough money to get rich. But how much of your income *should* you save? Ten percent? Twelve and a half percent? An hour a day? Two hours? The realistic answer is "As much as you can." Saving something, even if it's just 5%, is much, much better than saving nothing. But if you want to know how much you ought to be Paying Yourself First to achieve your financial goals, use this formula as a basic guideline. Which choice is right for you?

EXERCISE
The Pay Yourself First Formula

How to use it: Decide what your goal is for retirement, then read the choices and choose which Pay Yourself First amount fits your goal and place a check mark next to it.

THE PAY YOURSELF FIRST FORMULA		
How much of your income should you save? That depends on your goals. To be . . .		**Your choice**
Rich enough to retire early	Pay Yourself First at least 20% of your gross income.	
Rich	Pay Yourself First 15% to 20% of your gross income.	
Upper middle class	Pay Yourself First 10% to 15% of your gross income.	
Middle class	Pay Yourself First 5% to 10% of your gross income.	
Poor	Think about Paying Yourself First, but don't actually do it.	
Dead broke	Don't Pay Yourself First. Spend more than you earn, borrow money you can't pay off, and live on credit cards.	

When you've finished the exercise: Now you have your Pay Yourself First goal. Next, you're going to work on reaching it!

TELL ME MORE!

In the next few chapters, you'll learn where to put your Pay Yourself First money and how to create a systematic savings plan that will never fail. But first, let's solidify what you've learned in this chapter by completing the Pay Yourself First Motivator.

KEY POINTS TO REMEMBER FROM THIS CHAPTER

- You can't get rich by budgeting.
- Paying Yourself First is the only sure way to get rich.
- You should be working at least one hour a day for yourself.
- Using pretax retirement accounts means saving 10% of your income will cost you a lot less from your take-home pay.

EXERCISE
The Pay Yourself First Motivator

How to use it: First, record the ways your eyes were opened by learning about Paying Yourself First. Next, jot down a to-do list of action steps for 24 hours and 7 days. Finally, list a few people with whom you want to share your new insights about paying yourself before creditors or Uncle Sam.

THE PAY YOURSELF FIRST MOTIVATOR

What is your biggest breakthrough from this chapter?

1	
2	
3	

What are the most important actions you want to take in the next 24 hours?

1	
2	
3	

What are the most important actions you want to take in the next 7 days?

1	
2	
3	

What from this chapter do you want to share with someone else in your life?	Why?
1	
2	
3	

When you've finished the exercise: Decide which of your action items you can tackle before tomorrow, then get going.

OK, you've made tremendous progress so far! In fact, just by getting to this point, you understand more about the mechanics of building wealth than most Americans. But now that you have the knowledge, it's time to take some action. So let's take what we know and look at how you'll turn your Latte Factor and Pay Yourself First into wealth by Making It Automatic.

CHAPTER FOUR

NOW MAKE IT AUTOMATIC

You remember Jim and Sue McIntyre. They became Automatic Millionaires by setting up a Pay Yourself First system that automatically saved a percentage of their incomes for more than 30 years. Because their plan was automated, they never had to write checks. Implementing their plan took no time and no discipline. Once they decided how much to Pay Themselves First, the plan took care of itself.

So the most important thing you can do is to begin Paying Yourself First—RIGHT NOW. Even if you can only set aside 1% of your income, fine. Do it. Start saving. Once you do, you're on your way to becoming an Automatic Millionaire.

In this chapter, you're going to learn how to Pay Yourself First a percentage of your income . . . and you're going to be like the McIntyres and Make It Automatic. The secret is really no secret at all: It's your company retirement plan.

IF YOU HAVE A RETIREMENT PLAN AT WORK, USE IT!

You've heard of the most common retirement accounts: the 401(k) plan, and the 403(b) plan for health care and education workers. There are six great reasons to enroll in one of these plans if you're eligible:

1. You don't pay a cent in income tax on the money you put into the plan or on the returns it earns until you take it out after you retire.
2. As of 2005, you can put up to $14,000 a year into one of these accounts if you're under age 50, and more if you're older.
3. You can make your payroll deductions automatic.
4. There are usually no fees.
5. Your employer may *match* some or all of your contributions.
6. You'll enjoy the miracle of compound interest.

EXERCISE
What Do You Know About Your Retirement Plan?

I'm always surprised how little some people know about their company retirement program. Time to see what you know. Do you know who manages it? How much your company's matching contribution is? This exercise will show you exactly what you know and what you need to find out.

How to use it: Fill in the information you know today. You may know this information by heart or can find it in an accessible file. If you don't know, don't guess. Find out, then come back and fill the blanks in later.

WHAT DO YOU KNOW ABOUT YOUR RETIREMENT PLAN?	
Type of plan—401(k), 403(b), etc.	
Who is your company benefits officer?	
What is the benefits officer's phone number or e-mail address?	
Are you contributing to your company plan?	
If so, how much and how often?	
What percentage of your contribution does your employer match?	
Are there any fees for enrolling in your plan?	
What company manages the investments in the plan?	
What do others say about your company plan?	

When you've finished the exercise: Now you know what information you need to gather to have a total picture of your retirement plan options. And that's crucial as you move forward and increase your contribution level!

THE BEAUTY OF GETTING PAID
BEFORE THE IRS

What makes these tax-deferred retirement plans so fantastic is that when you contribute to a 401(k) or 403(b) plan, the percentage of your pay that is deposited into your retirement account is taken from your pretax earnings. *You get paid before the government gets to collect its taxes.* Talk about Paying Yourself First! That's a terrific advantage over other kinds of investing, as these tables show:

	401(k) Retirement Plan (pretax)	Regular taxable investment
Gross income	$1.00	$1.00
Minus taxes	−0	−30%
Amount available to invest	$1.00	$.70
Annual return	10%	10%
Balance after one year	**$1.10**	**$.77**
Gains taxable?	No	Yes

After one year, you'd have 43% more money in your account by avoiding paying taxes on your investment! Over 30 years, that's hundreds of thousands of dollars. But it gets better. Let's say your employer matches part of your 401(k) contribution:

	401(k) Retirement Plan with Employer Match	Regular taxable investment
Gross income	$1.00	$1.00
Minus taxes	−0	−30%
Amount available to invest	$1.00	$.70
Typical employer match	25%	NA
Total amount invested	$1.25	$.70
Annual return	10%	10%
Balance after one year	**$1.38**	**$.77**
Gains taxable?	No	Yes

By investing in your tax-deferred retirement account and getting even a 25% matching employer contribution, you'd earn nearly *80%* more money every year! That's a huge, life-changing difference in your Automatic Millionaire plan. If you're not sure if your employer matches employee retirement contributions, *ask*. If they do, celebrate.

IF YOU'RE NOT SURE YOU'RE ENROLLED, CALL AT THE END OF THIS CHAPTER

According to a 2002 survey by PlanSponsor.com, 25% of American workers who are eligible for retirement accounts haven't signed up.

Don't risk being one of them. If you're not sure you're enrolled in your company's retirement plan, when you finish this chapter, call the benefits officer at your company and ask if you're enrolled. If you're not, get a retirement enrollment kit sent to you *immediately*. If you work for a large company, you might also be able to get the information on their web site. And if you got the kit when you were hired but set it aside, get it out and read it. Do it now.

AN AUTOMATIC MILLIONAIRE SUCCESS STORY

Following the steps in *The Automatic Millionaire* inspired me to pay off my debt in its entirety, revamp my ailing credit history, and save toward retirement, when before, I'd been living paycheck to paycheck for most of my life. Even though now I'm experiencing another layoff, I have the luxury of choosing from good options, and can support myself for a couple of years if necessary. Thank you for the information and inspiration.

Kristin Wall
Stockton, CA

PICK A PERCENTAGE . . . THEN DO A LITTLE MORE

As we've discussed, you should be saving at least one hour's worth of income each day. That should come to about 10% of your gross income. If you can, start your retirement account deductions at 10%. If that's too much, start lower and work up to 10% or even higher. Anything is better than nothing.

At the same time, be ambitious. This is your future. If you think you can start out by investing 4%, be aggressive and save 6%. If your instincts tell you 10%, go for 12%. People tell me time and time again that when they stretch, they can't even feel the difference in their wallets. But they will certainly see it in their increased retirement savings.

BRAINSTORMING BREAK

What could you do to max out your retirement plan?

NOW MAX IT OUT!

The fastest way to become rich is to MAX OUT YOUR PLAN. In other words, make the largest contribution you can, according to your plan rules. This is the maximum allowable under current tax law:

401(K), 403(B), AND 457 PLAN CONTRIBUTION LIMITS		
Year	Maximum Allowable (age 49 and younger)	Maximum Allowable (age 50 and older)
2005	$14,000	$18,000
2006	$15,000	$20,000

Note: After 2006, contribution increases will be adjusted for inflation in $500 increases.

Use this table as a guide, but check with your company's benefits officer. Some companies set their maximum contribution lower than the federal limit. So don't guess. Check with your benefits office and recheck every January to take full advantage of any increases in the limit.

THE SINGLE BIGGEST INVESTMENT MISTAKE YOU CAN MAKE

Not using your retirement plan and not maxing it out is the single biggest investment mistake you can ever make. I can't overemphasize how important it is to max out your retirement plan. It really can make the difference between a retirement of total freedom and one of ceaseless worry.

Jim and Sue McIntyre told me about two couples they knew who were automating their 401(k) contributions. One couple maxed their contribution out right away, putting away 15% of their incomes. The other lowballed their contribution (putting 4% away) and promised to increase it "someday." *Well, someday never came.* Both couples had similar incomes and lived in the same neighborhood. However, when everybody retired, the couple who had maxed out their contribution had accumulated more than $500,000 more than the other couple.

Don't wait for "someday." Maximize your retirement contribution now. Take this one action and you will have changed your financial future for the better—guaranteed.

AUTOMATION PLUS COMPOUND
INTEREST EQUALS REAL WEALTH

Once you've maxed out your pretax retirement account and gotten any "free money" that your employer will contribute, compound interest makes your Automatic Millionaire fortune possible.

Over time, money compounds.
Over a lot of time, money compounds dramatically!

Don't take my word for it. The following table shows you how the miracle of compounding turns small but consistent savings into real wealth.

SAVINGS GROWTH OF $100 DEPOSITED MONTHLY								
Depending on the rate of return, putting just $100 a month into an interest-bearing account and then letting it compound can generate a surprisingly large nest egg.								
Interest Rate	5 Years	10 Years	15 Years	20 Years	25 Years	30 Years	35 Years	40 Years
$100/mo invested at 2.0%	$6,315	$13,294	$21,006	$29,529	$38,947	$49,355	$60,856	$73,566
$100/mo invested at 3.0%	6,481	14,009	22,754	32,912	44,712	58,419	74,342	92,837
$100/mo invested at 4.0%	6,652	14,774	24,691	36,800	51,584	69,636	91,678	118,590
$100/mo invested at 5.0%	6,829	15,593	26,840	41,275	59,799	83,573	114,083	153,238
$100/mo invested at 6.0%	7,012	16,470	29,227	49,435	69,646	100,954	143,183	200,145
$100/mo invested at 7.0%	7,201	17,409	31,881	52,397	81,480	122,709	181,156	264,012
$100/mo invested at 8.0%	7,397	18,417	34,835	59,295	95,737	150,030	230,918	351,428
$100/mo invested at 9.0%	7,599	19,497	38,124	67,290	112,953	184,447	296,385	471,643
$100/mo invested at 10.0%	7,808	20,655	41,792	76,570	133,789	227,933	382,828	637,678
$100/mo invested at 11.0%	8,025	21,899	45,886	87,357	159,058	283,023	497,347	867,896
$100/mo invested at 12.0%	8,249	23,234	50,458	99,915	189,764	352,991	649,527	1,188,242

See what compounding can do? Over 40 years, saving $100 a month costs you $48,000. From that savings, even at a 6% rate of return, you end up with $200,145! And at the 12% rate (very possible if you invest wisely), you end up with a nest egg worth nearly *25 times* your contribution amount!

I'm telling you, compounding is incredible.

AN AUTOMATIC MILLIONAIRE SUCCESS STORY

Immediately after reading *The Automatic Millionaire*, I called our brokerage company to send me the forms so that we can automatically deposit $250 per month in each of our IRAs and $500 per month into our money market account. I then called our mortgage company and switched to a biweekly payment plan. My husband then increased his 401(k) from 6% to 10% and we also started automatic deposits into our children's 529 Plans. I advised our daughter to have 50% of her paycheck directly deposited into a money market account.

David . . . in one weekend you have changed my life. I will recommend your books to anyone who will listen! What you say makes so much sense. Thank you and God bless you!

Beth Wolf
Menomonee Falls, WI

YOUR COMPANY DOESN'T HAVE A RETIREMENT PLAN? OPEN AN IRA

The Individual Retirement Account is a personal retirement plan that almost anyone can set up in about an hour at a bank, brokerage firm, or even on the Internet. Like a 401(k) or 403(b), an IRA is a holding tank for your money; you decide the vehicles to invest it in, such as mutual funds. Once you open your IRA, you can make tax-deferred contributions of up to $3,000 a year ($3,500 if you're 50 or older).

There are two types of IRAs to consider: the traditional IRA and the Roth IRA. Both have benefited from recent tax law changes and are stronger now than at any time in the last 20 years. But which is right for you?

TRADITIONAL IRA VS. ROTH IRA

You don't pay income tax on the dollars you contribute to a traditional IRA.* But you are liable for income tax on all monies you withdraw from the account, and you must begin to withdraw your money by the time you reach age 70½.

With a Roth IRA, you pay income tax on the money you contribute (in other words, your contributions can't be deducted from your taxable income). And there are income limits on a Roth IRA.† But if the money has been in the account for at least five years and you are over 59½, you pay no taxes when you withdraw it.

WHICH IRA IS RIGHT FOR YOU?

Unless your income is high enough to put the Roth off-limits, which IRA you choose will probably depend on whether you want your tax benefits now or later. Complete this worksheet to help you determine which IRA is a better fit for you:

EXERCISE
Traditional IRA vs. Roth IRA

How to use it: Take this brief quiz to determine which IRA is better suited for your income and goals. For the question about tax deductions on traditional IRAs, talk to your company benefits officer or your tax advisor.

---

*A traditional IRA may not be tax-deductible if you are covered by an employer plan. Please check IRS Publication #590 for details.

†If you earn less than $95,000 a year ($150,000 for married couples), you can contribute up to $3,000 a year. If you earn more than that, the amount you can put in is reduced. If you earn more than $110,000 (or $160,000 for married couples), you cannot use a Roth IRA. Visit www.irs.gov for updates and most current information regarding income qualifications for retirement accounts.

TRADITIONAL IRA VS. ROTH IRA	
1 When do you want your tax deduction?	a) Now b) On withdrawal
2 Do you earn:	a) $95,000+ a year* b) Less than $95,000 a year *If you earn more than $95,000, the amount you can contribute to a Roth IRA is reduced.
3 If you are enrolled in your company retirement plan, can you still get a tax deduction for a traditional IRA?	a) Yes b) No
Your answers: If you answered "a" to the questions, then a traditional IRA is probably the best choice for you. If you answered "b," then a Roth IRA might be the better choice.	

When you've finished the exercise: Now that you know which IRA is probably best for you, take steps to confirm it. Talk to a financial advisor or broker, or to the retirement specialist at a mutual fund company, and get all the specifics. Then open that IRA and start saving. If you'd like to do further research into the benefits and limitations of investing in a Roth IRA, you can get great information at **www.rothira.com.**

OPENING YOUR IRA ACCOUNT

Hundreds of banks, brokerage firms, and mutual fund companies can open your IRA or Roth IRA for you. I've chosen these six because they make the process very quick and easy: They're large firms with secure, full-featured online services and friendly, expert phone support. They can help you set up and automate your IRA in minutes.

- **Sharebuilder**
  866-747-2537
  www.sharebuilder.com

- **TD Waterhouse**
  800-934-4448
  www.tdwaterhouse.com

- **INGDirect.com**
  800-ING-DIRECT
  www.ingdirect.com

- **Transamerica Goal Tender**
  877-GTENDER
  www.transgoaltender.com

- **Ameritrade**
  800-669-3900
  www.ameritrade.com

- **Vanguard**
  800-869-8623
  www.vanguard.com

IF YOU'D RATHER TALK TO A REAL PERSON . . .

If you're not comfortable opening a retirement account online, no problem. When you go into a bank or brokerage to open your IRA, be sure to tell the banker or broker assisting you that you want to open a systematic investment plan.

There are plenty of top-flight banks and brokerage firms that can answer all your questions and help you choose the type of account and the individual investments that are right for you. Here are some full-service financial service companies to consider:

FULL-SERVICE BROKERAGE FIRMS

- **AG Edwards**
  877-835-7877
  www.agedwards.com

- **American Express**
  800-297-7378
  www.americanexpress.com

- **Charles Schwab**
  866-855-6770
  www.schwab.com

- **Edward Jones**
  314-515-2000
  www.edwardjones.com

- **Fidelity Investments**
  800-FIDELITY
  www.fidelity.com

- **Merrill Lynch**
  800-MERRILL
  www.ml.com

- **Morgan Stanley**
  212-761-4000
  www.morganstanley.com

- **Salomon Smith Barney**
  212-428-5200
  www.smithbarney.com

NATIONAL BANKS

- **Bank of America**
  800-242-2632
  www.bankofamerica.com

- **Citibank**
  800-248-4472
  www.citibank.com

- **Washington Mutual**
  800-788-7000
  www.wamu.com

SETTING UP YOUR AUTOMATIC INVESTMENT PLAN

OPTION ONE: PAYROLL DEDUCTION

Payroll deduction is the best way to set up an automatic investment plan. If your employer is set up to do this, you will be asked to fill out a form that asks you for the account information they need to transfer the funds each pay period. That means you'll need to open your IRA and get the appropriate account number and routing information. Some banks and brokerages will even handle the process for you, working directly with your employer. Be sure to ask about this.

OPTION TWO: CHECKING ACCOUNT DEDUCTION

If your employer doesn't offer payroll deduction, ask them if they provide automatic **direct deposit** of your paycheck into your bank account. If they do, you can arrange to have money automatically transferred from your checking account to your retirement account at the end of each month.

Virtually any bank or brokerage that offers IRAs is equipped to set up this kind of automatic transfer for you. The great thing about checking-account deduction is its flexibility: You can change or increase your deduction with a phone call.

> ### THE INCREDIBLY SIMPLE WAY TO
> ### AUTOMATE ALL YOUR FINANCES
>
> Once you open an online bill pay account, your bills go directly to your bank, which scans them and sends them to you via a secure web site. To pay your bills, you just click a button, and the funds are automatically deducted from the account you choose. I've been using online bill pay for years to pay all my personal and business bills. It's a wonderful time-saver, and it's usually free from banks.
>
> One of the best things about this service is that you can use it to send money wherever you like automatically. So if you want to deposit $75 a week into your retirement fund, online bill pay can do it for you automatically without your doing a thing.

CAN I REALLY GET RICH
SAVING JUST $3,000 A YEAR?

As of 2004, the maximum amount you can contribute to your IRA was $3,000 a year if you're under age 50 (if you're over 50, it's $3,500). That works out to $250 a month, or about $12 per working day. So unless you make less than $12 an hour, max out your IRA contribution. Remember, you're working at least an hour a day for yourself now!

But can you really get rich saving $3,000 a year? Yes, thanks to the power of compound interest. If today you started putting $250 a month into an IRA that earned an annual return of 10%, in 40 years you'd have a retirement nest egg worth nearly $1.6 million. In only 25 years, you'd have about $335,000.

SELF-EMPLOYED GOLD MINE #1:
THE JOY OF SEP

The real payoff comes when you're self-employed; you can save a lot more per year. The Simplified Employee Pension, or SEP, is a retirement account for a self-employed person. You can now contribute as much as 25% of your gross income to a SEP IRA up to a maximum of $41,000 (the amount is adjusted for inflation each year). You have to work hard to max out that retirement account!

If you're self-employed, run—don't walk—to the nearest bank or brokerage and open a SEP IRA today. The only tricky part of the process is Making It Automatic. If you draw a regular paycheck, this isn't a problem. Simply set up your payroll system to transfer contributions automatically to your SEP IRA.

If you don't draw a regular salary, each time you take money from your business account, you transfer an extra 10% to your SEP IRA. But since this may be impossible to automate, consider paying yourself a salary so you can automate transfers from your checking account.

Remember, the key is to Make It Automatic.

SELF-EMPLOYED GOLD MINE #2: ONE-PERSON 401(K)/PROFIT-SHARING PLAN

This amazing option lets the owner of a one-person business open a 401(k) plan for as little as $100. Once you've done that, you can invest up to 100% of the first $12,000 you earn (more in later years), and up to another 25% of your income. As of 2004, the combined maximum you could invest was just over $41,000 per year, with annual increases for inflation.

Want to know why business owners can get rich faster than employees?

- Say you earn $50,000 as a self-employed person.
- With a One-Person 401(k)/Profit-Sharing Plan, you could invest the first $12,000 you earned in the 401(k) account.
- Then you could put another 25%, or $12,500, into the profit-sharing portion.
- That's $24,500 in pretax savings on a $50,000 income!

If you're self-employed, call your local financial company today (as most are now offering it). Here are three specific mutual fund companies that offer these plans directly: Aim Funds (**www.aimfunds.com**), John Hancock Funds (**www.jhancock.com**), and Pioneer Funds (**www.pioneerfunds.com**). My wife and I set up one of these plans for our business in 2002, and it took 20 minutes (we did it through our payroll provider—if you have a payroll provider or benefits group, ask them if they can help you). Also, most mutual fund companies and brokerage firms are now offering these plans.

EXERCISE
The Plan Qualifier Checklist

This exercise consolidates what we've discussed so far and should help you pull together all your retirement account information.

How to use it: Just go down the list of the different retirement savings plans and check off the ones that you qualify to invest in. In the last column, write down your maximum annual contribution for each account that you qualify for.

THE PLAN QUALIFIER CHECKLIST		
Retirement plan	**Do you qualify?** (circle one)	**Maximum account you can contribute per year**
Employer 401(k)	YES/NO	$_____
Employer 403(b)	YES/NO	$_____
Traditional IRA	YES/NO	$_____
Roth IRA	YES/NO	$_____
SEP IRA	YES/NO	$_____
One-Person 401(k)	YES/NO	$_____

When you've finished the exercise: Use the Retirement Account Setup Guide on page 80 to help you keep track of what you learn from your retirement account research.

AN AUTOMATIC MILLIONAIRE SUCCESS STORY

I have already reinstated my automated children's education IRAs, [started making] extra payments on my mortgage, and I'm in the process of increasing my company IRA contributions. I was doing these things in the past, but put a temporary hold on them. *The Automatic Millionaire* prompted me to start them back up now, and also to increase my contributions. I have noticed a huge difference in what I spend on a daily basis. I have significantly reduced my Latte Factor, because I think about that $3.50 per mocha or $4 movie rental and late fee. I don't cut them out altogether (that wouldn't be fun); I simply make them rewards, rather than casual purchases.

David, you are truly making a difference, and I am carrying the torch to those I can help as well.

Brian Nottingham
Akron, OH

EXERCISE
The Automatic Millionaire
Retirement Account Setup Guide

How to use it: Make 6 to 10 photocopies of the worksheet and have them beside you as you call banks and brokerages about setting up an IRA, SEP, or One-Person 401(k) account. You'll find key questions to ask each one, as well as space for writing down the answers. Fill out a worksheet for each bank or brokerage you call and use the information to help you choose the company that's right for you.

THE AUTOMATIC MILLIONAIRE
RETIREMENT ACCOUNT SETUP GUIDE

Name of Bank/Brokerage:

Type of account you're inquiring about: IRA, Roth, SEP, One-Person 401(k)	
Can I set up a systematic investment program where you automatically take money out of my checking account on a regular basis and invest it in my retirement account?	
What is the minimum initial investment?	
Will you lower the initial investment amount if I arrange for regular automatic contributions?	
Who manages the investments within this retirement account? What is their contact information?	

Their Rate:

Their Fees:

Contact Person:

Phone Number:

When you've finished the exercise: When you've finished your calls, use this information to decide where you're going to open your retirement account . . . then open it and congratulate yourself.

HOW SHOULD YOU INVEST YOUR RETIREMENT MONEY? DIVERSIFY!

Whether you have a 401(k), IRA, or SEP, it's just a tax-deferred holding tank for your money. You still have to decide where to invest. The investment determines whether you'll make 10% or 1% on your money over time.

The best advice: Don't put all your eggs in one basket. Diversify—invest your money in a variety of places so you're not depending on one kind of investment to perform well. Within your retirement account, you should build a diversified portfolio of stocks, bonds, and cash investments. By spreading your money around, you'll be investing the way all the smartest investors do.

EXERCISE
Part One—Where Is My Money Invested?

I see this all the time: couples who don't have the slightest idea what kinds of investments their retirement savings are in. I think that's crazy. If you're going to make the savvy decisions you need to become an Automatic Millionaire, you need to know where your money is.

How to use it: Just review account statements from your broker, bank, or company benefits manager and fill in the percentages.

PART ONE: WHERE IS MY MONEY INVESTED?		
Is your Pay Yourself First nest egg invested in the right place? Fill in the blanks below to figure out where you've put your money.		
How much of my nest egg is in:		
Cash and bonds?	_____	%
Income investments?	_____	%
Growth investments?	_____	%
Growth & income investments?	_____	%
Aggressive growth investments?	_____	%
	Total: 100%	

When you've finished the exercise: Congratulations! Now that you know where your money is, you can move it around to make it work harder for you. In a few pages, Part Two of this exercise will help you do exactly that!

THE POWER OF THE PYRAMID

The Automatic Millionaire Investment Pyramid is a wonderful tool for helping you determine where to invest your money and how much to put into each investment. It's based on two principles:

1. Your money should be invested in a combination of stocks, bonds, and cash.
2. Your portfolio should change over time as your life situation changes.

As you'll see, the pyramid divides your financial life into four distinct periods: the "Getting Started" years, the "Making Money" years, the preretirement years, and the retirement years. For each period, the pyramid suggests the percentage of your total retirement portfolio that should be allocated to each of five types of investments. The investments, from safest to riskiest, are:

- Cash and bonds
- Income investments
- Growth investments
- Growth and income investments
- Aggressive growth investments

THE AUTOMATIC MILLIONAIRE INVESTMENT PYRAMID

TEENS TO THIRTIES (The "Getting Started" Years)

Situation and goals
- Aggressive
- Growing net worth
- Very long-term outlook
- Willing to take a fair amount of risk

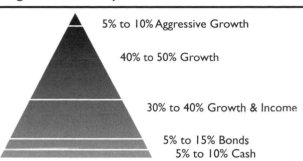

5% to 10% Aggressive Growth

40% to 50% Growth

30% to 40% Growth & Income

5% to 15% Bonds
5% to 10% Cash

THIRTIES TO FIFTIES (The "Making Money" Years)

Situation and goals
- Ten or more years to retirement
- Building net worth
- Willing to take risk
- Not needing investment income

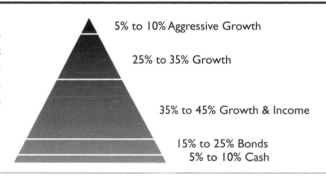

5% to 10% Aggressive Growth

25% to 35% Growth

35% to 45% Growth & Income

15% to 25% Bonds
5% to 10% Cash

FIFTIES TO MID-SIXTIES (The "Preretirement" Years)

Situation and goals
- Less than ten years to retirement
- Typically high-income years with fewer financial responsibilities
- Willing to take some risk but wanting less volatility

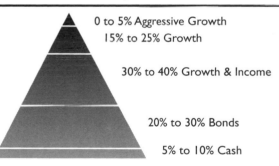

0 to 5% Aggressive Growth
15% to 25% Growth

30% to 40% Growth & Income

20% to 30% Bonds

5% to 10% Cash

SIXTIES AND UP (The "Retirement" Years)

Situation and goals
- Enjoying retirement or very close to retiring
- Protecting net worth
- Preferring less risk

0 to 5% Aggressive Growth

10% to 20% Growth

30% to 40% Growth & Income

25% to 35% Bonds

10% to 15% Cash

HOW THE PYRAMID WORKS

The base of the pyramid rests on the safest investments. As you work your way up, the investments get more risky with the potential for higher return. The older you get, the less risky your investment mix should be. When you're younger, you have decades to ride out a bad stock market or recover a loss. When you're near retirement, you don't have that time. It's an effective principle that all savvy investors use.

Rather than investing in a lot of individual stocks, I recommend investing in mutual funds. Mutual funds give you professional money management, ease of use, and they're diversified between many different stocks. You can start investing in some funds with as little as $25.

EXERCISE
Part Two—Where Should My Money Be Invested?

Now that you've seen the Automatic Millionaire Pyramid, you may have some different ideas about investing your retirement nest egg. This is where you'll write them down so you can act on them.

How to use it: Using the information from the Pyramid, reallocate your money according to what's best for your stage of life.

PART TWO: WHERE SHOULD MY MONEY BE INVESTED?
Based on what you learned about risk from the Automatic Millionaire Pyramid, where should you be investing your money?
My nest egg should be in:
Cash and bonds: _____ %
Income investments: _____ %
Growth investments: _____ %
Growth & income investments: _____ %
Aggressive growth investments: _____ %
Total: 100%

When you've finished the exercise: You're doing fantastic! You've made some of the most important decisions an investor can ever make, and you've done it without a stockbroker by your side. Now you're ready to call your brokerage and move your assets where they should be.

MY FAVORITE WEB SITES FOR RESEARCHING MUTUAL FUNDS, STOCKS, AND FINANCE

The Internet is the best tool ever for digging up information about mutual funds, stocks, bonds, financial markets, and much more. I think it's safe to say that whatever you want, you can find it. Take some time and read through some of these sites; they have some amazing tools that for the most part are free:

- www.morningstar.com
- finance.yahoo.com
- www.mfea.com
- www.smartmoney.com
- www.nyse.com
- www.nasdaq.com
- www.edgaronline.com

SUPER-SIMPLE, ONE-STOP INVESTING

If mutual funds (and different types of investing categories, like growth, growth and income, aggressive growth, etc.) confuse you, don't worry. Many company retirement plans offer a simple choice that gives you a prepackaged portfolio of diversified investments. The funds are chosen for you; you don't even have to figure out what percentage of your money should go to stocks versus bonds.

This one-stop-shopping plan can be called an *asset-allocation fund*, a *fund of funds*, or a *life stage fund*. If your fund options have years in their name, such as 2030, select the year closest to your projected retirement year. You might also be offered a *balanced fund*. This typically gives you professional management with 60% stock and 40% bonds.

The wonderful thing about these funds is that they do all the work for you. They give you the right mix of cash, bonds, and stocks in one fund, making investing incredibly easy. You don't even need to work for a company to get them. You can invest your IRA, Roth IRA, or SEP IRA in the same kinds of professionally managed asset-allocation funds.

WHAT'S YOUR RISK TOLERANCE?

Before you invest in anything, it's vital to know how much risk you're willing to tolerate. Remember, the higher the risk, the higher the potential reward, but also the higher potential for loss.

Investing toward becoming an Automatic Millionaire should be exciting and energizing, not worrisome and stressful. So before you make any investment decisions, know how much risk you're comfortable with. There's no right answer here; what matters is that you enjoy the journey toward wealth and independence.

EXERCISE
The Automatic Millionaire Risk-Tolerance Test

How to use it: Simply answer the questions honestly based on how the concept of investing makes you *feel*. Then review what your results mean at the bottom.

THE AUTOMATIC MILLIONAIRE RISK-TOLERANCE TEST

The higher the risk, the higher the return. But how much risk are you willing to tolerate in your investments? Take this test and discover your personal comfort zone.

		(circle one)
1	Do you get stressed by the daily ups and downs of the securities markets?	YES NO
2	Are you unfamiliar with investing?	YES NO
3	Do you consider yourself more of a "saver" than an "investor"?	YES NO
4	Do you constantly worry about losing your assets in a short time?	YES NO
5	Are you investing for a goal less than 10 years away?	YES NO
6	If you took a 25% short-term loss, would you change your plan?	YES NO

Results:

If you answered "Yes" to four or more of these questions, you are more than likely a conservative investor and should probably allocate more of your retirement money toward lower-risk investments, with less invested in more volatile, higher-risk areas. A balanced approach to investing (60% stocks and 40% bonds) may be the appropriate approach for you to take. When in doubt, talk to a financial advisor at your bank or brokerage, or your company benefits officer, to find out how you should change your investments. Most financial service firms, banks, and mutual fund companies offer a "computerized risk tolerance" questionnaire that you can take in minutes.

When you've finished the exercise: Do you realize how much you've learned about investing in this chapter? About the mechanics and the psychology of it? You're well on your way to membership in the club of Automatic Millionaires!

IF YOU STILL WANT TO KNOW MORE ABOUT RETIREMENT ACCOUNTS . . .

You can get virtually any question answered in one of two enormously useful pamphlets available free from the IRS. Go to **www.irs.gov** and request Publication #590 ("Individual Retirement Arrangements") and Publication #560 ("Retirement Plans for Small Businesses"). You can download them right from the Internet.

If you don't have Internet access, you can call the IRS toll-free at 800-829-3676 to request the reports. You can also call toll-free for all sorts of financial assistance. The number is 800-829-1040. To find out what free services are available, request Publication #910 ("Guide to Free Tax Services"). You see, the government really *does* want you to save money tax-free by making pre-tax contributions to a qualified retirement plan.

WHATEVER YOU DO, MAKE IT AUTOMATIC

Right now your mind might be juggling mutual funds, SEP IRAs, and a lot of other investment information. But whatever retirement accounts you select, and whatever mix of investments you choose, don't forget the single most important task you have:

Make It Automatic!

While you're at it, funnel at least 10% of your income into a tax-deferred retirement account and max it out as soon as possible. With what you've learned so far, you can make your retirement planning both incredibly simple and incredibly effective. So use what you know and make it happen!

> ## KEY POINTS TO REMEMBER FROM THIS CHAPTER
>
> - If you're not enrolled in your company retirement account, enroll immediately.
> - Compound interest turns small amounts of money into real wealth over time.
> - Even if you're invested in your 401(k) or other retirement account, you can still open a traditional or Roth IRA.
> - You should invest in a way that suits your tolerance for risk.
> - Wherever you invest, Make It Automatic.

EXERCISE
The Make It Automatic Motivator

How to use it: You know how to use these Motivators by now. First, write down the things that really blew your mind from the Make It Automatic chapter. Next, list action items for 24 hours and 7 days out. Then list whom you'll share this information with. It's too good to keep to yourself!

THE MAKE IT AUTOMATIC MOTIVATOR

What is your biggest breakthrough from this chapter?

1

2

3

What are the most important actions you want to take in the next 24 hours?

1

2

3

What are the most important actions you want to take in the next 7 days?

1

2

3

What from this chapter do you want to share with someone else in your life?	Why?
1	
2	
3	

When you've finished the exercise: Start making calls. Call your employer. Call your broker. Call your bank. Open the accounts you need. Make them automatic. In a few hours, you can change your life!

When you sat down and opened *The Automatic Millionaire Workbook,* did you think you could have come this far in a couple of hours? You have! Now for the next part: how to buy yourself financial security for a rainy day.

CHAPTER FIVE

AUTOMATE FOR A RAINY DAY

If you Pay Yourself First and Make It Automatic, you can do nothing else and you will already have assured yourself a bright financial future. But what about today? This chapter will answer two important questions:

1. How much should you put aside for a "rainy day"?
2. Where should you put it?

HOW WELL DO YOU SLEEP AT NIGHT?

No matter how well you plan or how positively you think, things can always go wrong. People lose their jobs, develop health problems, get divorced. The economy can go sour, the stock market can drop—things can change fast. Stuff happens.

Automatic Millionaires prepare for change. When they hit a bump in the road, they don't have to borrow against their future or raid their Pay Yourself First money to survive. They've thought ahead. That's what you're going to do.

Have you put yourself in a position to sleep well at night? Take this test and find out:

EXERCISE
The "Sleep Well at Night" Factor

How to use it: This is an easy one. Just fill in your expenses and savings; go back to the Income Statement in Chapter One if you need to.

THE "SLEEP WELL AT NIGHT" FACTOR	
a My current total monthly expenses:	$
b What I currently have saved in a checking or money market account:	$
c This equals how many months of emergency expenses? (b ÷ a)	

When you've finished the exercise: Are you surprised at how vulnerable you are? Or do you have more emergency money saved than you realized? Either way, it's time to save systematically and make your money work for you. Ready?

PREPARING FOR A "RAINY DAY"

How many months' worth of expenses do you have saved? Do you feel comfortable with what you have saved?

The average American has less than three months' worth of expenses set aside. In my personal experience as a financial advisor, I've found that most people don't even have that much. Our culture is one of spend, not save. That's why we're breaking records for personal bankruptcies, and I predict we're going to be doing the same with foreclosures on personal residences before long.

Think about it: How close are you to disaster if you or your spouse lost your paycheck? How long would it take for you to be upside down financially?

BRAINSTORMING BREAK

What kinds of emergencies could happen in your life?
How much money would it take to get through them?

BUILD AN EMERGENCY BASKET OF CASH

I'm going to show you how to make sure that *never* happens to you. As part of becoming an Automatic Millionaire, you're going to build an emergency basket of cash AUTOMATICALLY.

You may never plan on losing your job or becoming disabled. But stuff happens. The way you live your life without worrying about it—and the way you protect yourself if something does happen—is by surrounding yourself with a cushion of money.

THE THREE RULES OF EMERGENCY MONEY

RULE 1. DECIDE HOW BIG A CUSHION YOU NEED.

To be a real Automatic Millionaire, I believe you should strive to have at least three months' worth of expenses saved. Estimate how much you spend each month on your essential expenses (housing, food, utilities, car, etc.), multiply it by three, and you have your emergency savings goal.

Should you save more than three months' worth of expenses? Of course, if you can. In my previous books, I've recommended that you put aside anywhere from 3 to 24 months' worth of expenses. But it depends on your situation. What do you need to sleep well at night? Are you thinking about quitting your job and changing careers? Are you in a business that's experiencing a lot of layoffs? When it comes to emergency savings, the Automatic Millionaire rule is *save as much as you need to give yourself peace of mind.*

Personally, I think saving a year's worth of expenses is a great goal. It gives you incredible freedom. If you get laid off, you don't have to worry about finding a new job right away. If someone gets sick, you can take time off to be a caregiver. And if the spirit moves you, you can really say, "Enough with the job" and try something new.

Take a few minutes right now and complete this exercise to figure out the minimum amount you should save for your Sleep Well at Night Fund:

> ## EXERCISE
> ## The Rainy Day Fund Builder

How to use it: In Part 1, write down all your monthly survival expenses. Survival expenses are things you need to keep a roof over your head, keep clothes on your back, keep food in your cupboards, keep your family healthy, and keep from defaulting on your debts. Cable TV and dinners out are NOT survival expenses. When you have them all listed, add them up.

Then comes the tricky part: your risk factors. In Part 2, take an honest look at how vulnerable you are. Are you or your spouse in a job where you might be laid off at any time? Does someone have a medical problem that could result in big hospital bills? Could your pipes burst at any moment? If you have risk factors like these, you can see why you need to plan for them and add to your monthly emergency money. When you've added any risk factors, add that percentage to your regular monthly expenses, and that's the size of the rainy day money cushion you need to save each month.

In Part 3, simply ask yourself how many months' cushion you need to have peace of mind. Multiply that number by your rainy day money amount—that should be your emergency savings goal.

THE RAINY DAY FUND BUILDER	
Step 1: Your Monthly Survival Expenses	
Rent or mortgage	$
Utilities (electricity, gas, water, sewer, trash)	$
Auto (car payments, fuel, maintenance)	$
Food	$
Clothing	$
Insurance	$
Health care (doctor visits, co-pays, etc.)	$
Other expenses	$
Total Expenses	$
Step 2: Your Risk Factors	
If a wage earner is in a volatile business with lots of layoffs, add 10% to Expenses	%
If a member of your family has a chronic serious health problem, add 10%	%
If your car or your home's plumbing, electrical, or structure is in serious need of repair, add 10%	%
Total % Added to Expenses	%
Total Monthly Rainy Day Money	$
Step 3: How Much Should You Save?	
How many months of emergency expenses do you need to have peace of mind?	
Your Total Monthly Rainy Day Money	$
Months × Rainy Day Money	$
Total Money You Need to Save (copy from line above)	$

When you've finished the exercise: Now you have your goal. Great. Next, start making plans on what to save and how to save to reach it. And that's exactly what we're going to do now.

RULE 2: DON'T TOUCH IT.

The main reason most people don't have any emergency money is that they spend it on things that aren't emergencies. I want you to think of your emergency money as a fire extinguisher on the wall in an office building. The sign above it says, "In case of fire, break glass." It doesn't say, "If you smell smoke, break glass." You wouldn't grab the fire extinguisher if you dropped a lit cigarette on the rug; you'd stamp it out with your foot.

Think of your emergency fund the same way. The imaginary sign on it doesn't say, "In case you really need a new dress for the party . . ." or "In case the latest golf club has just gone on sale . . ." It's only for real emergencies. What is an emergency?

> *An emergency is something that threatens your survival, not your comfort.*

That means someone loses a job, somebody gets sick and runs up a huge hospital bill, your house burns down, you get sued, and so on. If the possible consequences include defaulting on debts, foreclosure, or bankruptcy, it's an emergency. Otherwise, it's just an inconvenience.

What's your idea of an emergency? Will you be able to resist temptation to tap your rainy day fund for something that's not critical? This exercise will help you decide.

EXERCISE
The Emergency Stoplight System

If you've never thought about what a real emergency is, this exercise will make you think. Many people think an emergency is when they can't have what they want. They're wrong. An emergency is something that can ruin your financial life. Five minutes with this exercise and you'll be thinking differently about what equals a crisis and what's just a headache.

How to use it: First, take a look at the situations I've listed and how I rate them. "Red" situations are emergencies; they are what you've saved your rainy day money for. "Yellow" situations may be important, but they probably won't threaten your survival. And "Green" situations are hardly worth mentioning. They're minor inconveniences.

Next, write down situations you're likely to encounter in your life and rate them Red, Yellow, or Green.

THE EMERGENCY STOPLIGHT SYSTEM			
When is an emergency really not an emergency? Use this exercise to clarify the situations where tapping your emergency fund is OK.			
KEY: **Red** = It's an emergency; use the money. **Yellow** = It's questionable unless the situation could lead to a bigger crisis. Use your judgment. For example, if your refrigerator breaks down but you have a backup in the garage that you can use until the repairman comes, it's not an emergency. **Green** = It's not an emergency. Don't touch.			
The Situation	**Red**	**Yellow**	**Green**
The refrigerator breaks down.		X	
The mortgage is in default.	X		
The kids want the latest video game.			X
Write and "light" your own situations	**Red**	**Yellow**	**Green**

When you've finished the exercise: Remember, if something is just an inconvenience, do not tap your emergency fund. The only justifiable reason to spend that money is if something threatens your survival.

RULE 3. PUT IT IN THE RIGHT PLACE.

I once conducted a seminar where I talked about the importance of setting money aside for emergencies. During it, a man named Bob raised his hand and told me he had $60,000 plus some gold coins saved for emergencies, and that he and his wife had expenses of only about $2,000 per month. This is a huge cushion.

I asked Bob how much interest he was earning on this money, and the answer floored me. "I'm not earning any," he said. "I've got it buried in my backyard."

I was stunned into silence. So was everyone else. Then someone in the front row turned to Bob and said, "Out of curiosity, where exactly do you live?"

That broke the seminar up completely. People were laughing so hard they had tears running down their faces.

AN AUTOMATIC MILLIONAIRE SUCCESS STORY

After I read *The Automatic Millionaire*, my husband and I set our goal to own our own home by the end of the year. Only two short months later, we closed on a house with 4½ acres and a pond! We are paying extra on the mortgage every month to pay it off early as you suggested. We are also paying off our other debt while still managing to save! My husband recently changed jobs and will be able to enroll in the company 401(k) program. I am an Independent Beauty Consultant with Mary Kay and I have started giving your book as a gift to my new team members. It doesn't do much good making money if you don't manage it wisely! Thank you. You are truly an answer to my prayers!

Lucinda McConney
Sandersville, GA

NOT EARNING INTEREST IS AS BAD AS BACKYARD BURIAL

The issue, however, was very serious. No way was Bob one of a kind. I don't think there are millions of Americans with small fortunes buried in their backyards, but I'm sure there are millions out there putting aside their rainy day money without earning a dime of interest on it.

Doing that is almost as bad as what Bob did. Remember, Automatic Millionaires make their money work for them. Yours should be working for you.

DON'T LET BANKS GET RICH
OFF YOUR SAVINGS

Banks love when people set up rainy day funds, because most people put their emergency money in savings or checking accounts that pay little or no interest. In fact, these accounts can actually cost you money—monthly fees, ATM charges, check fees, and so on. Meanwhile, the bank gets to use your money for loans without paying you a dime for the privilege.

I think if a bank is going to use your money to make money, they should pay you for it. Whatever you do with your emergency money, always put it in an account where it will grow. I suggest this: Put it in a money market account that pays reasonable interest.

A money market account is one of the simplest, most secure choices for someone who wants to put aside cash and earn a decent return. When you deposit in a money market, you're actually buying shares in a mutual fund that invests in short-term government bonds and highly rated corporate bonds—the safest investments around.

Best of all, the minimum amount you need to open a money market has dropped. It used to be as much as $10,000. But now there are money markets you can open for as little as $1,000—and some for as little as one dollar. You heard me right: *one dollar*.

SHOP FOR A RATE LIKE YOU'D
SHOP FOR A CAR

Today there are thousands of money market accounts out there, and the cost and quality vary widely. So just as you'd shop around for a car, shop around for a money market rate. Ask questions and don't be afraid to play competitors against one another.

The most important variable is, of course, the interest rate. Not only is there a huge variation from bank to bank, but rates change daily. These days, rates are at historic lows. In fact, even though they've begun to rise at the time of this writing, you'd still be lucky to get a rate over 1.5% for a balance under $25,000. But still, that's better than nothing, and rates can only go up.

So you need to become a smart rate shopper. Some of your best sources for rate information:

SOURCES FOR RATE INFORMATION		
The Wall Street Journal	www.wsj.com	The nation's most trusted source for financial news.
Investor's Business Daily	www.investors.com	One of the oldest publications on investments and financial markets.
Barron's	www.barrons.com	Another deeply respected financial periodical.
BankRate	www.bankrate.com	This wonderful web site is a clearinghouse of interest rate information for different banks from all over the country, and it also tells you the minimum deposit required by each. Even better, you can sort banks by state, which is useful since some states allow tax-free money market and checking accounts.

CALL YOUR BANK

Once you know the rate landscape, it's time to call the bank that currently has your rainy day money. Ask them how much interest your money is earning. If it's zero, ask them if they offer money market accounts. If they do, ask what they pay and what it takes to open one. Then compare the rate to what you've seen elsewhere.

If your bank doesn't offer money markets or you can get a better combination of rates and opening balance somewhere else, it's time to move your rainy day cash from your current bank to a money market at another institution.

FOR THE BEST DEAL, CALL A BROKERAGE FIRM

Brokerage firms will usually give you a higher-yielding money market than a bank. These are some of the most reputable brokerage houses I've found for opening a money market account. There are many more, of course, but this list will help you make a sound decision:

BROKERAGE FIRMS CHECKLIST					
Name	**Min. Deposit**	**Phone Number**	**Web Address**	**Notes**	**Called**
ING Direct	None	800-ING-DIRECT	www.ingdirect.com	Some of the highest rates around, and you can open your account and arrange for an automatic money transfer online in a few minutes.	
Edward Jones	None	314-515-2000	www.edwardjones.com	Works closely with small investors and has more than 8,000 branches around the country.	
E*TRADE Bank	$1,000	800-ETBANK1	www.etrade.com	Be sure to look at the E*TRADE Bank Money Market Account Plus.	
Morgan Stanley	$1,000	866-742-6669	www.morganstanley.com	One of the world's largest full-service financial firms, with a full menu of brokerage services.	
Fidelity Investments	$2,500	800-FIDELITY	www.fidelity.com	A leading provider of mutual funds, with thousands of branch locations nationwide to help you.	
Vanguard	$3,000	800-992-8327	www.vanguard.com	Offers one of the lowest-cost, highest-yielding money market funds around, if you can get past the higher initial deposit.	
Charles Schwab	$10,000	800-225-8570	www.schwab.com	Schwab has offices throughout the country and gives you all the tools to do your own investing, provided you can handle the very high minimum deposit.	

EXERCISE
The Money Market Rate Shopper's Guide

How to use it: Make 6 to 10 photocopies of the worksheet and have them beside you as you call banks and brokerages about setting up an automatic money market account. You'll find the six key questions to ask each one, as well as space for writing down their rate and fees. Fill out the worksheet for each bank or brokerage you call, and use the information to help you choose the one that's right for you.

THE MONEY MARKET RATE SHOPPER'S GUIDE

Name of Bank/Brokerage:	
What's the minimum to invest?	
Can I set up a systematic investment program where you automatically take money out of my checking account on a regular basis and invest it in a money market account?	
If I set up a systematic investment plan, will you lower the minimum to invest?	
Do you offer federally insured accounts? What's the rate on your insured money market accounts vs. your regular money market accounts?	
Does the account come with check-writing privileges, and if so, what's the smallest check you can write? Does it come with an ATM card?	
Do you charge a low-balance fee if my balance goes below a certain minimum? If so, what is it?	

Their Rate:

Their Fees:

Contact Person:

Phone Number:

When you've finished the exercise: You've got the information to put the banks and brokerages on the spot. You know the inside scoop on their products, which gives *you* the power. Time to use it and get the best possible return on your money.

GETTING AROUND THOSE NASTY MINIMUMS

Often the biggest obstacle for someone trying to open a money market account is the minimum deposit. Fortunately, there's often a way around it. Just ask the brokerage if they offer a money market fund that takes systematic investments. Most do, and as long as you sign a form agreeing to make regular monthly investments, they'll let you open a brokerage account to invest in a money market with as little as $100. But you probably won't get the ATM or check-writing privileges that you'll get with a standard money market account.

A piece of advice: Don't keep your rainy day money in the same account you use to pay your regular bills. That makes it too easy to dip into your emergency money for monthly expenses—and before you know it, it's gone. Keep your day-to-day and rainy day accounts separate and "lead yourself not into temptation."

BRAINSTORMING BREAK

What did you learn from your calls to banks and brokerages?

NOW ... MAKE IT AUTOMATIC!

Remember, if you make your financial affairs automatic, you can't fail. So once you've opened your money market account and set up a system to invest something in it every month, before you know it you'll have your emergency fund. Here's the process I suggest following:

STEP ONE

Do your research using the resources on page 103 and your own information, then select the bank or brokerage that gives you the best mix of high interest rate, low fees, and manageable opening deposit. If you have more than $1,000 to deposit, you should be able to find one that gives you an ATM card and check-writing privileges. If you don't have that much, open an account without those options.

STEP TWO

Check to see if your employer offers payroll deduction (most will). If they will, you can arrange to have part of your paycheck deposited to your rainy day account. Just give your benefits office the account number.

STEP THREE

Decide how much to save each month. I suggest that you strive to put aside 5% of your take-home pay each month. If your employer wants a specific amount, get out your calculator and figure out the dollar amount. You can always change it when your salary goes up.

STEP FOUR

If your employer won't do payroll deduction into your money market account, you can arrange to have your checking account automatically fund your money market account. You can do this in one of two ways: Instruct the bank where you have your checking account to automatically transfer a specific dollar amount to your money market account every two weeks; or instruct the bank or brokerage that has your money market fund to do a "systematic withdrawal" from your checking account, in which money is taken from your checking account on a specific day each month.

EXERCISE
The "Make It Automatic" Checklist

Use this checklist to make it easier and more convenient to put the four steps into action.

How to use it: Just take each step as described, check it off, and write down your results.

THE "MAKE IT AUTOMATIC" CHECKLIST		
Step	✓	**Results**
1. Select the bank or brokerage that gives you the best mix of rate, fees, and opening deposit.		
2. Does your employer offer payroll deductions? Arrange to have part of your paycheck deposited to your rainy day account.		
3. Decide how much to save each month.		
4. If your employer won't do payroll deduction, choose an automatic transfer from your checking account or a systematic withdrawal from your checking account.		

When you've finished the exercise: Just like that, you're automated.

AN AUTOMATIC MILLIONAIRE SUCCESS STORY

David, I just finished reading your book and came away with a plan. My wife is 40 and I am 39. We have three boys 8, 5, and 18 months, and this is what we have made automatic:

- Fall of 2003 we moved into our new house, paying off about $40K in credit card and loan debt with the proceeds from our sale. By the end of May 2004 we will have paid the last $1,500 in debt, leaving just a car payment and mortgage.
- We both automatically contribute about 10% each to our 401(k) plans, for a total of $1,000 a month. We currently have about $32K in our plan and hope to retire comfortably at 65, maybe sooner.

There are two things I would like to accomplish: reopening a Roth IRA that I stopped, and starting a money market account for a rainy day. I hope we are on the right track after years and years of just making it. I see the light at the end of the tunnel.

Don and Meg King
Coatesville, PA

LET THE GOVERNMENT HELP YOU
AUTOMATE FOR A RAINY DAY

I want to share one more really safe, simple way to automate your rainy day fund: government bonds. The U.S. government has made it easy to buy bonds online, and if you're looking for a safe investment that's guaranteed by the full faith and credit of the U.S. government, consider U.S. savings bonds.

WWW.TREASURYDIRECT.GOV

This is a terrific web site that lets you quickly and easily invest as little as $50 a month in two types of U.S. savings bonds: I-Bonds and EE Bonds, also known as Inflation Bonds and Patriot Bonds.

Inflation Bonds

Inflation bonds are called that because their earnings rate is indexed to inflation. That means twice a year the rate is changed based on the Consumer Price Index, so if inflation goes up (as it did at the time of this writing), your rate of return goes up as well. (As of mid-2004, I-Bonds were paying about 3.4%.)

Other features of I-Bonds:
- The minimum purchase is just $50. The maximum you can buy is $30,000.
- Interest is added monthly.
- I-Bonds are sold at face value, so when you buy $100 worth, it costs you $100 in cash.
- I-Bonds earn interest for up to 30 years.
- You can sell an I-Bond after one year, though if you sell before five years, you will be penalized three months' worth of interest.

Patriot Bonds

Patriot Bonds are savings bonds that were issued after the September 11 terrorist attack. They pay 90% of the return you'd get from a five-year treasury note. As of mid-2004, EE Bonds were paying about 2.85%.

Other features of EE Bonds:

- Interest is added monthly and compounded twice per year.
- They are sold at 50% of face value. That means that to buy $100 in Patriot Bonds, you actually spend just $50. Then, when they come due, you can cash them in for the full $100 value.
- You can sell an EE Bond after one year, but as with the I-Bond, you face penalties if you sell within five years.

AN AUTOMATIC MILLIONAIRE SUCCESS STORY

I discovered today that I'm only contributing 5% to my 401(k)! At that rate I'll be working until I'm 90. I will be increasing it to 10% next enrollment period. I figure with my raise plus a little more I won't even miss it. A month or two ago I started the process of purchasing my first home! There are so many great programs out there for first time homebuyers. If more people my age (30) knew this they would all be doing it. I am working a second job to save more money for the down payment. After that, I'm going to open a Roth IRA.

Thank you so much—keep up the good work.

Alyssa Sand
Webster, NY

AUTOMATE YOUR BOND PURCHASE

It's really easy to automate your bond buying:

THE AUTOMATIC BOND-BUYING CHECKLIST		
Step	**✓**	**Results**
1. Go to **www.savingsbonds.gov** or **www.treasurydirect.gov**.		
2. Do any additional research into Inflation Bonds and Patriot Bonds, such as historical rates of return or tax advantages.		
3. Choose your bond type and click on "Open an Account." There you can set up your account and choose to buy bonds through automatic withdrawals from your checking or savings account or using payroll deduction.		
4. Set up the account online, or you can print the forms and fax them.		

I get asked a lot where I would keep my rainy day money—in a money market account or in U.S. savings bonds. My answer is: both. Just like with stocks, it's better to diversify. Money markets let you get to your money more easily, without a penalty. But right now, bonds pay a higher rate of return, because they are longer-term investments. So my suggestion: Put some of your money in both.

IF YOU'RE IN DEBT . . .

. . . then things should change. For people with big credit card balances, I recommend building up one month's worth of emergency money, then concentrating on paying down the debt. Why? Because it doesn't make sense to have money earning 1% in a money market fund while you're paying 20% on credit card debt. Paying that debt off is like earning 20% on your money.

Later on in *The Automatic Millionaire Workbook*, we'll go through a plan that will help you pay off your credit cards faster, lower your interest rate, and get out of debt. Then you can start building that emergency fund.

KEY POINTS TO REMEMBER FROM THIS CHAPTER

- Emergency money is your cushion against unexpected misfortune.
- Put your rainy day money into a money market account to earn interest.
- Talk to banks, talk to brokerages, and shop for a rate carefully.

EXERCISE
The Automate for a Rainy Day Motivator

How to use it: Write down the lessons that opened your eyes and the steps you want to take within the next day and the next week.

THE AUTOMATE FOR A RAINY DAY MOTIVATOR

What is your biggest breakthrough from this chapter?

1

2

3

What are the most important actions you want to take in the next 24 hours?

1

2

3

What are the most important actions you want to take in the next 7 days?

1

2

3

What from this chapter do you want to share with someone else in your life?	Why?
1	
2	
3	

When you've finished the exercise: You're in the major leagues of financial strategy now! You've done more than 99% of the people you know will ever do to protect their present while ensuring their future. Give yourself a hand and enjoy what you've accomplished so far.

Do you realize how far you've come in such a short time? You've already learned how to Pay Yourself First, Make It Automatic, and save for a rainy day. You're very close to being where most Americans only dream of being: in a place where you never have to worry about money again.

Now, get ready, because we're going to look at the real secret to getting rich: owning your own home.

CHAPTER SIX

AUTOMATIC DEBT-FREE HOMEOWNERSHIP

You can't get rich renting. It's really that simple. If you're currently renting, I know it's hard to hear this, but please listen. According to the U.S. Federal Reserve Survey of Consumers and Finance, the average renter in 2001 had a median net worth of $4,800—while the average homeowner had a median net worth of over $171,000. *When you rent, you make your landlord rich—and you keep yourself poor.* That's why in this chapter we're going to look at the third of my three secrets to long-term financial security: owning your own home and paying it off early.

LANDLORDS GET RICH, RENTERS STAY POOR

As a renter, you can easily spend at least half a million dollars or more on rent over 30 years ($1,500 per month over 30 years equals $540,000)! And in the end, you wind up with exactly what you started with—nothing. Your landlord makes out like a bandit, while you throw money down a bottomless pit.

The sad part is that most renters could spend the same amount every month on a mortgage payment and own their own home. They could pay down their mortgage each month and watch their investment go up in value while they enjoy the tax breaks that the government gives to homeowners. Consider this an Automatic Millionaire law:

You won't build wealth until you become your own landlord.

If you are currently renting, buying your own home (a house or a condo, it doesn't matter) should be a top financial priority. But is it possible to make buying a home and paying it off early easy? Yes, and the exercises in this chapter are going to show you exactly how.

AN AUTOMATIC MILLIONAIRE SUCCESS STORY

Just a quick note to let you know how incredibly easy it has been to put your concepts from *The Automatic Millionaire* into reality!

It took about 5 minutes to set up an automatic money market account at my bank. We already had our mortgage payment automatically deducted every month but it took a 30-second conversation to set up an additional principal payment every month. It only added a little over $100 to our payment and is well worth it. It took me longer to get through their voice mail menu than it did to set this up!

Thanks, David—this really does work.

Lee Ann Snyder
Roswell, GA

DEBT-FREE HOMEOWNERSHIP MADE EASY

When I met Jim and Sue McIntyre, I was impressed by how much they had benefited from buying a house and paying it off early. Remember, by buying their first home when they were young and accelerating the payments a little, they had it paid off in less than 20 years and were able to buy another home and pay it off early, too.

As a result, Jim and Sue were able to retire with no debt and a net worth of well over a million dollars. You can do the same thing.

But first, let's look at six of the top reasons why buying a home is such a great decision.

SIX REASONS WHY HOMES ARE THE BEST INVESTMENT YOU'LL EVER MAKE

REASON #1: FORCED SAVINGS

Homeownership is a kind of mandatory savings program: It forces you to make a contribution each month in the form of a mortgage payment, or you could lose your home. The best thing is, you're making one of the greatest investments around: home equity, one of the few investments that in the long term nearly always goes up in value.

REASON #2: LEVERAGE

Leverage means using borrowed money to increase your financial returns. When you buy a home, you get leverage. Let's say you buy a $250,000 home with a down payment of 20%. So you're putting in $50,000 of your own money and borrowing the rest. Since you've put in one-fifth of the purchase price, you've got five to one leverage.

Now, if in a few years your home increases in value to $300,000, that $50,000 increase means you've doubled your money, because you put in only $50,000 to begin with. The more your home goes up in value, the greater return you earn on your initial investment. That's the power of leverage.

AN AUTOMATIC MILLIONAIRE SUCCESS STORY

I was raised by parents who think the way Jim and Sue McIntyre do . . . I am extremely grateful they raised me the way they did. When my husband asked me to read your book, I thought to myself, "What could I possibly learn from this that I don't already know?" After reading your book I've gained knowledge of paying a mortgage biweekly and also of IRAs and Roth IRAs . . . Thanks for helping me realize I could still do more. You really helped me and my husband. I am putting those lattes into my mortgage payment.

Dawn Francesconi
Bartlett, IL

REASON #3: OPM

OPM stands for "other people's money." I just love this phrase and philosophy, because it's true and it works. Rich people always invest with other people's money. If you want to know the ultimate reason the rich get richer, it's OPM. And that's exactly what you're doing when you buy a home—using the bank's money to get rich. Meanwhile, your own money can be working for you someplace else, like compounding in a retirement account.

REASON #4: TAX BREAKS

Uncle Sam loves homeowners. That's why he lets you deduct your mortgage interest from your income taxes. If you're in the 30% tax bracket, the government is basically subsidizing almost a third of your mortgage payment, especially early on when you're paying mostly interest. That's an incredible incentive to buy a home.

REASON #5: PRIDE

It feels great to own a home, to be part of a community, and to put down roots. Owning a home is security.

REASON #6: IT'S A PROVEN GREAT INVESTMENT

For most people, the biggest and best investment they'll make is their home. No matter what you hear about real estate "bubbles" (like we're hearing about these days), real estate prices almost always go up long-term. In fact, since 1968, real estate investments have averaged an annual return of 6.3%.

BRAINSTORMING BREAK

What's been stopping you from buying a home, and what can you do about it?

DON'T BE SCARED BY
THE DOWN PAYMENT

The most common reason people put off buying a home is that they think they can't pull together a down payment. Many people think they need to come up with tens of thousands of dollars in cash before they can get a mortgage. This is just not true. There are dozens of programs sponsored by developers, lenders, and the government that can enable first-time buyers to finance up to 100% of a home's purchase price. You'll start out with little equity and have larger payments, but as long as you can afford them, this is a wonderful way to get out of renting and into owning fast!

AGENCIES AND COMPANIES THAT CAN HELP YOU BUY A HOME		
U.S. Department of Housing and Urban Development	www.hud.gov	HUD offers all kinds of assistance to would-be homebuyers, including grants to help first-timers.
National Council of State Housing Finance Agencies	www.ncsha.org	The NCSHA web site contains links to a huge number of loan programs for first-time buyers, many that allow you to buy a home for less than 5% down.
Federal National Mortgage Association (Fannie Mae)	www.fanniemae.com	This is a private company that operates under a congressional charter to encourage and assist homeownership for low-, middle-, and moderate-income Americans. Also check out the related site www.homepath.com.
Federal Home Loan Mortgage Corporation (Freddie Mac)	www.freddiemac.com	Since 1970, Freddie Mac has financed 26 million home purchases. It does not make loans, but instead provides the financing that allows lenders to provide affordable terms to would-be buyers.

Those are the agencies. Now here are some of the best loan programs out there for first-time buyers:

LOAN PROGRAMS TO CONSIDER		
Federal Housing Administration (FHA)	www.fhaloan.com	The FHA is an agency within HUD that specializes in giving lenders mortgage insurance, enabling them to lend to first-time buyers who might otherwise have trouble qualifying for a loan. FHA loans can be a godsend to first-timers: You could buy a home for as little as a 3% down payment.
Veterans Administration (VA Loans)	www.valoans.com	The U.S. Department of Veterans Affairs offers a program that guarantees loans made to veterans of the U.S. armed services.
State Bond Loans	www.ncsha.org	Most states offer individual bond programs designed to help people get into their first home.

EXERCISE
How Much Can You Put Down?

There are programs that will help you buy a home with no money down. But in general, the bigger the down payment you can make on the home you're buying, the better your loan terms will be. Putting more down also means starting out with more equity and having smaller monthly payments. I tell people to try to save 10% of their take-home income toward a home down payment. That's a healthy rate that you should be able to manage. If you can't, save as much as you can. This is the most important investment you will ever make.

My basic rule is: Put down whatever you can save in a year without taking away from your Pay Yourself First plan. If you can only save $5,000 in a year, fine. That's the core of your down payment. As we discussed, there are plenty of programs designed to help first-time buyers get into homes with very little down.

How to use it: Write down every source you will have available for saving down payment money over the next year. For sources like tax refunds or bonuses, make your best estimate based on what you've received in the past. At the bottom, add up your total down payment potential.

HOW MUCH CAN YOU PUT DOWN?	
Your current savings	$
10% of your take-home income (or as much as you can manage)	$
Year-end bonuses	$
Tax refunds	$
Gifts from friends or family	$
Other sources	$
Total amount you could save in one year:	$

When you've finished the exercise: What is your one-year savings total? Make it a goal. One year from finishing this book, you will have your down payment.

SAVING YOUR DOWN PAYMENT

Right now, saving thousands of dollars for a down payment might seem like climbing a mountain. But like everything else in the Automatic Millionaire plan, it's easy if you're systematic and you Make It Automatic. The key is to set up a dedicated down payment savings account, something you can't touch for any reason. Then automate monthly deposits into that account and watch your down payment start to grow.

EXERCISE
The Down Payment Start-up Plan

How to use it: You're going to save 10% of your take-home income, or more, toward your down payment this year. Fill in the blanks to calculate just how much you need to save each month. Then set up an account you can keep that money in.

THE DOWN PAYMENT START-UP PLAN	
a. Your annual income	$
b. What is 10% of that amount? (Or more, if you can manage)	$
c. What you need to save each month (b ÷ 12)	$

Now open your down payment savings account:

Step 1: Contact banks to find out about their best checking accounts. Most will have something like a "Platinum" or "Premium" account that pays decent interest with a high balance. You can also open a money market account, just as you did for your rainy day savings.

My bank: _____

Step 2: Transfer whatever you already have saved toward a down payment to that new account and record it below.

Starting amount: $ _____

Step 3: Arrange to have your monthly savings amount (c from above) automatically transferred from your regular checking account to your down payment account at the same time each month.

Amount transferred each month: $ _____

When you've finished the exercise: You've got your automatic down payment savings plan in place. You're on your way to becoming a homeowner.

BRAINSTORMING BREAK

What can you do to reduce your expenses or increase your income to help save the money you'll need to reach your down payment goal?

BUT CAN I AFFORD A HOME?

I'd like to pose this question another way: How can you afford to keep wasting rent and never own anything? Most people don't realize that the money they spend on rent today could pay for a home tomorrow.

The historically low interest rates of 2003 and 2004 may be behind us, but rates are still very, very low. That means that basically, for every $1,000 a month you spend on rent, you could pay for $125,000 worth of mortgage payment, including taxes and insurance. So if your rent is currently $2,000 a month, for the same amount of money you could make payments on a $250,000 mortgage. In most of the country, that buys you a lot of house!

HOW MUCH HOME CAN I AFFORD?

Lenders decide whether or not to give you a loan based on your ability to repay it, of course—and that ability has a lot to do with the percentage of your total income the loan payments make up. For example, the FHA's rule of thumb is that most people can afford to spend 29% of their gross income on housing expenses up to 41% if they have no other debt.

So what does that mean for you with your income? Take a look at this table to get some basic and useful answers:

Annual Gross Income	Monthly Gross	29% of Gross	41% of Gross
$20,000	$1,667	$483	$683
$30,000	$2,500	$725	$1,025
$40,000	$3,333	$967	$1,367
$50,000	$4,176	$1,208	$1,712
$60,000	$5,000	$1,450	$2,050
$70,000	$5,833	$1,692	$2,391
$80,000	$6,667	$1,933	$2,733
$90,000	$7,500	$2,175	$3,075
$100,000	$8,333	$2,417	$3,417

You can keep doing the math on your own if you make more than $100,000 a year, but you get the picture. If you make $50,000 a year, you should be able to swing a $1,208 monthly mortgage payment—unless you have crippling debt (which we'll get to later). What would that payment buy you? That's an excellent question, and it's answered by the next table:

TYPICAL MORTGAGE PAYMENTS (WITH $0 DOWN)							
Monthly payments (principal and interest) for a 30-year, fixed-rate mortgage. Taxes, insurance not included.							
Mortgage Amount	5.0%	5.5%	6.0%	6.5%	7.0%	7.5%	8.0%
$100,000	$537	$568	$600	$632	$668	$699	$734
$150,000	$805	$852	$899	$948	$998	$1,048	$1,100
$200,000	$1,074	$1,136	$1,199	$1,264	$1,331	$1,398	$1,468
$250,000	$1,342	$1,419	$1,499	$1,580	$1,663	$1,748	$1,834
$300,000	$1,610	$1,703	$1,799	$1,896	$1,996	$2,098	$2,201
$350,000	$1,879	$1,987	$2,098	$2,212	$2,329	$2,447	$2,568
$400,000	$2,147	$2,271	$2,398	$2,528	$2,661	$2,797	$2,935
$450,000	$2,415	$2,555	$2,698	$2,844	$2,994	$3,146	$3,302
$500,000	$2,684	$2,839	$2,998	$3,160	$3,327	$3,496	$3,665

THE KEY TO SUCCESS: GET THE FINANCING RIGHT

As you can see, there's a big difference between a mortgage payment at 5% and one at 8%. It can be the difference between buying a $150,000 home and a $200,000 home. So now we're going to look at the most important part of buying a home and paying it off automatically: getting the right kind of mortgage.

There are many kinds of mortgages, and each one has its advantages and disadvantages. Here are some places where you can begin to get useful information about the different types of mortgages available:

WEB SITES FOR FINDING AND FINANCING A HOME

- www.citimortgage.com
- www.eloan.com
- www.homebuying.about.com
- www.homebuyingguide.org
- www.homepath.com
- www.lendingtree.com
- www.pueblo.gsa.gov
- www.quickenloan.com
- www.realtor.com
- www.smartmoney.com/home/buying

WHICH MORTGAGE IS RIGHT FOR YOU?

As you'll see after even a few minutes of research, there are a lot of different kinds of mortgages. They're designed to be ideal for different kinds of buyers with different needs, and mortgages that are perfect for one type are probably bad for another.

DIFFERENT TYPES OF MORTGAGES				
Mortgage type	Features	Pros	Cons	This mortgage is great for ...
30-Year Fixed-Rate	Most common mortgage. The rate stays the same for the entire term.	Locks in your interest rate, so payments are the same each month. Easy to track, no surprises.	You're locked into your rate for 30 years unless you refinance, so you can't benefit from falling rates.	Conservative buyers who plan on staying in their homes for years, first-time buyers who need lower payments.
15-Year Fixed-Rate	Basically the same as the 30-year fixed, except the rate and mortgage are for 15 years.	You'll get a lower interest rate than on a 30-year mortgage, and you'll pay off your home in half the time.	Your loan is compressed into half the time of a 30-year loan, so payments are higher.	Committed savers who plan to be in the home for years, have low debt, and earn healthy incomes.
Short-Term Adjustable-Rate (five years or less)	Interest rates may be fixed for the first six months to a year of the loan. Then they change (as often as monthly) based on the prime rate.	You get a substantially lower interest rate, making your monthly payment much less than other loans.	If interest rates go up fast, you'll find your payments going up with them.	People who want to keep their payments low and build up equity in their homes. People who can handle risk and plan on being in the home for less than five years.
Intermediate Adjustable-Rate (often called a 3/1, 5/1, 7/1, or 10/1 ARM)	The interest rate locks in for a specific period, then adjusts annually or every six months based on the prime rate.	Pretty low rates.	Your rate is predictable only for a limited time. Then it can rise if rates rise.	People who don't mind risk, want low payments, and plan on staying in the house for only a few years. The longer you lock in the rate, the higher the payments and the lower the risk.

EXERCISE
Which Mortgage Is Right for You?

How to use it: Answer the four questions as best you can, writing down your responses in the boxes. Then go to the bottom to total up your score. The result will give you a clearer idea of which type of mortgage is the best fit for your income, temperament, and goals.

WHICH MORTGAGE IS RIGHT FOR YOU?	
1. How financially conservative are you?	a. Conservative b. Moderate c. A risk taker
2. How long would you stay in your home?	a. 30+ years b. 10–20 years c. Just a few years
3. After expenses, how much do you have left at the end of the month now?	a. $1,000+ b. A few hundred dollars c. Next to nothing
4. What is the total amount you owe on car loans, credit cards, and student loans?	a. Less than $3,000 b. $3,000–$7,500 c. $7,500+

Scoring: Give yourself 1 point for every a, 2 points for every b, and 3 points for every c. Add up your total to determine what type of loan might be a good fit for you.

- If you scored 4–6, you're an ideal candidate for a 30-year fixed mortgage, and if you have sufficient income, might even be perfect for a 15-year mortgage.

- If you scored 7–9, you're in the middle of the pack. A 30-year mortgage might be good for you . . . if you can get a great rate and have a decent down payment.

- If you scored 10–12, you should look at adjustable-rate mortgages to save yourself money.

When you've finished the exercise: Now you at least have a place to start your research. The next step: Talk with a mortgage broker, preferably someone you're referred to by a friend or family member. They're the best people to tell you the current programs that might be available to you.

WHEN A 30-YEAR MORTGAGE MAKES SENSE

People frequently ask me which type of mortgage I would select. My first choice for most people would be a 30-year fixed-rate mortgage. There are two reasons for this. First, they're conservative and simple, with no sudden rate changes to mess with your finances. And second, if rates are low as they are now, they're a great deal, because you're locked into that low rate no matter where rates go in the future.

What's a low rate? Historically, anything below 8%. But in recent years, rates have dipped well below 6% and flirted with 5%, which gives buyers incredible buying power. Rates change daily, so try **www.eloan.com** or **www.yahoo.com** to get quick information on where rates are right now.

HOW YOU CAN GET RIPPED OFF BY A 30-YEAR MORTGAGE

That's all the good news. Here's the bad news: You can easily get ripped off by a 30-year mortgage *if you actually take 30 years to pay it off.* Want to know what's at stake? If you don't already own a home, ask a good friend or family member to look at the closing paperwork for their mortgage. Near the top, you'll find two numbers: the amount the homebuyers financed when they bought the house, and the amount they will actually have paid the lender when they finally pay off the loan.

As you'll see, the second number is SUBSTANTIALLY larger, probably to the tune of several hundred thousand dollars. That's the effect of interest being paid over 30 years. For example, if you buy a home for $250,000 with a 30-year mortgage at 8%, you'll wind up paying about $660,000 in mortgage payments! Think about that. You just paid $660,000 for a $250,000 home! Where did the extra $410,000 go? To pay your interest—meaning it went right into your lender's pocket.

Banks and lenders love 30-year mortgages. Thirty-year mortgages make them very, very rich. Now, this wouldn't be as much of a problem if people stayed in their homes for all 30 years, because over that time most homes will double or even triple in value. But that's not what people do: Most live in their homes for less than 10 years. In fact, the average is five to seven years. Here's some scary math: If you live in a house for seven years and sell it, you will have paid down the principal on your loan by only about 4%! On average, *more than 90%* of your mortgage payments during the first 10 years of your loan go to pay interest. If you choose an interest-only mortgage (which I don't suggest), it's even less.

Just writing this makes me want to open a bank.

HOW TO SAVE A FORTUNE ON YOUR MORTGAGE

You can spend 30 years working for your bank and making the bankers rich. Or you can take a different road, follow the plan I'm about to share with you, and own your home faster while making your bank hate you. Pardon the joke, but you can laugh all the way to the bank.

The way to do this is simple: *Pay your mortgage off early.* Easier said than done? Not with my "secret" one-step system. Here's what you're going to do: Take your ordinary 30-year fixed-rate mortgage, then pay it down faster using a biweekly payment plan.

THE AUTOMATIC MILLIONAIRE BIWEEKLY MORTGAGE PAYMENT PLAN

Anyone can do this. You don't need a special mortgage. You simply take the mortgage you have and, instead of making one payment a month, you pay half your monthly payment every two weeks.

Why does this work? It's very simple. There are 52 weeks in a year, so when you make a payment every two weeks, you're making 26 half-payments—equal to 13 full monthly payments on your mortgage. So by the end of the year, you will have made one extra mortgage payment.

AN AUTOMATIC MILLIONAIRE SUCCESS STORY

I just called the bank and increased our biweekly mortgage payment by $64 per payment, which is hardly a huge amount . . . but it saved us 2 years and 8 months of payments!! From now on, every time my husband or I get a pay increase I will bump up that amount. Thanks so much! Now we will be mortgage-free by the time we are in our early 40s and maybe even sooner!

Kirsty Knudson
Calgary, Canada

HOW MUCH CAN THIS REALLY SAVE ME?

One extra payment. No big deal, right? Well, not unless you like saving lots of money. Depending on your interest rate, that extra payment can pay your mortgage off somewhere between 5 and 10 years early (the average is 7 years)! Why? Because when you pay your principal early, it reduces the interest you owe, actually reducing the cost of your loan overall.

If you're an average U.S. homeowner, you could save more than $100,000 over the life of your mortgage loan just by following this simple program. And what may be best of all, you would be debt-free up to a decade sooner, ready to retire perhaps 10 years earlier than you planned!

THE $119,000 DIFFERENCE

The numbers don't lie. This amortization table shows that if you took out a $250,000 mortgage loan for 30 years at 8% and paid it off monthly, you'd pay $410,388.12 in interest over the life of the loan. But if you paid it off biweekly, the same mortgage would cost you just $291,226.69 in interest—a savings of $119,000.

MONTHLY PAYMENTS VS. BIWEEKLY PAYMENTS

Principal=$250,000   Interest Rate=8.00%   Term=30 years

Monthly Payment: $1,834.41	Biweekly Payment: $917.21
Average Interest Each Month: $1,139.97 vs.	Average Interest Each Biweekly Period: $372.41
Total Interest: $410,388.12	Total Interest: $291,226.69

Year	Principal Balance (Monthly Payments)	Principal Balance (Biweekly Payments)	Year	Principal Balance (Monthly Payments)	Principal Balance (Biweekly Payments)
1	$247,911.59	$245,930.37	16	$185,047.69	$123,579.76
2	$245,649.84	$241,523.50	17	$177,568.27	$109,035.14
3	$243,200.37	$236,751.55	18	$169,468.06	$93,285.38
4	$240,547.60	$231,584.16	19	$160,695.50	$76,230.62
5	$237,674.64	$225,988.62	20	$151,194.91	$57,762.73
6	$234,563.23	$219,929.44	21	$140,905.72	$37,764.62
7	$231,193.58	$213,368.21	22	$129,762.54	$16,109.50
8	$227,544.25	$206,263.32	23	$117,694.48	$0.00
9	$223,592.02	$198,569.74	24	$104,624.78	$0.00
10	$219,311.76	$190,238.67	25	$90,470.30	$0.00
11	$214,676.24	$181,217.31	26	$75,141.00	$0.00
12	$209,655.98	$171,448.45	27	$58,539.38	$0.00
13	$204,219.03	$160,870.16	28	$40,559.83	$0.00
14	$198,330.82	$149,415.36	29	$21,087.99	$ 0.00
15	$191,953.90	$137,011.44	30	$0.00	$ 0.00
			Result:	Paid off in 30 years	Paid off in 23 years

Source: Bankrate.com "Biweekly Mortgage Payment Calculator"

BRAINSTORMING BREAK

How much could you save paying your mortgage off early?

Run your own numbers and see what you could save. Visit **www. finishrich.com**, click "Calculators," then "Mortgages," then "Get a biweekly mortgage payment plan." You'll be amazed at how much you can save and how much sense this plan makes.

HOW TO SET UP A BIWEEKLY PAYMENT PLAN

Biweekly payment plans aren't really a secret anymore. Banks know about them. So to set up a biweekly payment plan, just call your lender. Tell them you want to set up a plan to pay your mortgage on a biweekly basis and you want to know if they offer a plan to let you do that *automatically*. There's an excellent chance the lender or the company that holds your loan offers just such a program.

Some of the benefits of setting up an automatic biweekly mortgage payment program:

- It saves you tens or even hundreds of thousands in interest payments.
- It puts you on a strong forced-savings system.
- It fits in with your cash flow, because you pay your mortgage every two weeks, when you get paid.
- You'll never worry about late payments because your payments are automated.
- You'll pay your home off years earlier.

TWO SMART QUESTIONS YOU SHOULD ALWAYS ASK YOUR LENDER

1. **Can I make extra payments on my mortgage without penalty?**
   The answer should always be "yes." DO NOT sign up for any mortgage that has a prepayment penalty.
2. **If I send in extra money beyond my required mortgage payment, what do I need to do to make sure the extra money is used to pay down my principal?**
   ALWAYS ASK THIS QUESTION! Believe it or not, standard policy at most banks is to take extra payments and hold them in a non-interest-bearing account—not to use them to pay down your mortgage. The bank will

probably ask for a letter specifically requesting that the extra payment be applied to your principal (ask if they have a form letter to this effect). Some banks may ask you to send the extra 10% separately. If you're automated, that should be no big deal. Simply automate two fund transfers per month on the same day.

EXERCISE
The Lender Questionnaire

How to use it: Call any lender you're shopping for a mortgage loan, ask these two important questions, and write down the answers. What you learn will help you choose the right mortgage.

THE LENDER QUESTIONNAIRE		
Question	**Lender Name & Contact Person**	**Response**
Can I make extra payments on my mortgage without penalty?		
What do I need to do to make sure the extra money is used to pay down my principal?		

When you've finished the exercise: Cross off your list any lenders who didn't give you the right answers.

FINDING A BIWEEKLY MORTGAGE

If your mortgage is with one of the larger banks, they'll probably refer you to an outside company that runs special loan-payment programs for them. These companies will generally charge you a one-time setup fee ranging from $195 to $395, plus a transfer charge ranging from $2.50 to $6.95 every time you make an automatic biweekly payment. For that fee, they'll automate the entire process.

You should probably use the payment company your bank refers you to. After all, it's in their interest to make sure your payments are handled properly. One of the best known is called Paymap, which provides accelerated mortgage payment services for more than half a dozen of the nation's largest banks. You can find out more about Paymap at **www.paymap.com** or by calling 800-209-9700.

EXERCISE
The Biweekly Mortgage Questionnaire

There are four vital questions you should ask any service company before you sign up for their biweekly mortgage payment program. You're looking for a company that uses your money to pay down your principal, rather than holding on to it in an account.

How to use it: Use this exercise as a worksheet to track the answers you receive when you call banks or third-party companies about their biweekly mortgage payment plans. Make a copy of this worksheet for each call you make.

THE BIWEEKLY MORTGAGE QUESTIONNAIRE	
Bank or Third-Party Company:	
What do you do with my money when you get it?	
When do you actually fund the extra payments toward my mortgage?	
How much will it cost me to use the program?	
How much money will I save by doing a biweekly plan?	

When you've finished the exercise: Take any biweekly payment processors or banks whose answers you didn't like and cross them off your list. You've made your shopping list a little shorter.

ISN'T THIS A LOT OF MONEY FOR SOMETHING I CAN DO MYSELF?

That's the thing: You can't just start paying your mortgage every two weeks on your own. Lenders won't let you. Their system is designed to process monthly mortgage payments; if you start sending them checks every two weeks, they'll just send one check back because they won't know what to do with it.

But is spending $2.50 every two weeks to pay your mortgage automatically really a waste of money? Based on the earlier example, you might save $119,000 over the life of your loan in interest payments. And with a company like Paymap, you'd spend around $2,000 to run this program over 22 years. That's still a savings (or a profit, if you like) of $117,000. Not bad.

Still reluctant to spend that kind of money? Think about what you get for it: an automatic system that pays your mortgage off early, tracks your payments so your lender doesn't miss crediting a payment, checks your statement for errors (which lenders make all the time), and helps you get debt-free years faster! To my mind, that's worth the price of a McDonald's dinner once a month . . . and better for you, too.

OK, YOU WANT TO DO THE SAME THING WITHOUT A FEE?

I hear this argument a lot, so let me share with you two "no-fee" approaches that can pretty much accomplish the same thing. Then I'll explain why, from experience, I don't think these "no-fee" approaches ultimately work.

NO-FEE APPROACH #1

Just add 10% to your mortgage payment each month. Using the example on page 133, let's say your monthly payment is $1,834. Ten percent of that is $183. If you added that amount to your regular monthly payment, you'd send your lender $2,017 each month—and you'd end up paying off your home in 22 years and saving about $129,000 over the life of your mortgage.

As with so much else in this book, the key to success with this approach is Making It Automatic. You don't want to depend on writing a check for 110% of your mortgage each month—it would be too easy to just pay your normal payment for any month where you had extra expenses. Avoid the excuse trap and have your 110% mortgage payment deducted from your checking account automatically.

NO-FEE APPROACH #2

Simply pick one month a year to pay your mortgage bill twice (I suggest doing it in May or June, just after you've received your tax refund). Don't send a check for twice the amount; that will just confuse your lender. Instead, write two checks for the regular monthly amount. Send one in with your mortgage coupon, and send the other with a note explaining that you want the entire amount applied to your principal. This will give you the same result as the 10% plan—and with no extra fees.

AN AUTOMATIC MILLIONAIRE SUCCESS STORY

Reading *The Automatic Millionaire* has already prompted me to make major changes. I have gathered all of my "errant" IRA Rollovers & 401(k)s into one place, I have AUTOMATED everything and have added my recent raise to my security account (making it retroactive, of course).

Thank you so very much for bringing this information to us in such a personable method. You are making a big difference in the quality of life for so many people!

Phyll Hurley
Littleton, CO

MAKE YOUR PLAN FAILURE-PROOF

While either of these no-fee approaches will work, the truth is that few people will actually make extra payments every single month, which is what it takes to pay your home off early and save all that interest money. So first decide whether you want to pay someone else to handle extra payments for you, or if you want to do it yourself.

WHAT IF I DON'T PLAN TO STAY IN MY HOME FOR 30 YEARS?

Is it worth it to pay off your mortgage early if you think you might only live in your home for 10 years? Yes. Remember, owning a home is forced savings. The faster you pay down your mortgage, the more equity you build up. When you sell, you cash out that equity and can use it to buy another home with a smaller mortgage, or increase your savings.

GETTING YOUR FINANCES IN SHAPE TO BUY

There are three key components to getting the right home loan. One is the home itself, which needs to be affordable and to pass the lender's appraisal. The second is the type of loan and the terms you get. The final one is your credit. And if you've never thought about buying a home before, that's the part that can get a little scary.

Lenders base the amount of money they're willing to lend you and the interest rate they charge you on your track record for paying back debt: your credit rating. You can check your rating at **www.myfico.com**, which, for a fee, will give you a detailed breakdown of your credit score according to the Fair Isaac & Co. (FICO) rating system. You can also get your credit scores from the three credit bureaus: Equifax (**www.exquifax.com**), Experian (**www.experian.com**), and Transunion (**www.transunion.com**).

But unless you have a perfect rating of 850, you can always improve your credit and your financial situation to make you more attractive to lenders. There are many steps you can take to reduce debt and make yourself a better risk.

EXERCISE
The Homebuyer Fitness Workout

How to use it: Describe your current situation—how much you have saved, how long before you want to be able to buy a house, and so on. There's no right or wrong answer to this exercise, only you getting the clearest picture possible of where you are today and what you need to do to be able to buy a home tomorrow.

THE HOMEBUYER FITNESS WORKOUT		
How long before you would like to buy a home?		
Your FICO score:		
Your partner's FICO score:		
What you have saved for a down payment:		
Workout # 1: Pay Debts on Time	Late payments damage your credit, and your outstanding debt reduces the size of the loan you can qualify for. Pay all your bills on time and pay off your highest-interest debt first.	Amount of debt you will pay off before shopping for a loan:
Workout # 2: Close Extra Credit Accounts	Too many open credit accounts can lower your credit scores. Get your credit history and close newer idle accounts. Keep older ones to show that you have a long credit history.	Accounts to close:
Workout # 3: Get Organized	You'll be asked to document your income and savings when you apply for a loan. Organize your bank statements, recent pay stubs, and tax returns.	Where are your records?
Workout # 4: Stay Employed	Lenders look for a solid employment history. If you're thinking about changing jobs, stop unless a new job could pay you a lot more.	How long have you been at your current job?
Workout # 5: Stop Spending, Start Saving	The amount you have to put down can influence the loan you can get. Stop spending more than you make and start saving automatically.	How much are you saving each month toward a down payment?

When you've finished the exercise: Start doing all the things you talk about in the exercise. Even better, try going to **www.myfico.com**, **www.equifax. com**, **www.experian.com**, or **www.transunion.com** for more information. You can purchase detailed information on your credit score, get a free estimate of your score, learn ways to improve your score, find out how to protect your financial information, and a lot more.

GET YOUR FINANCES IN SHAPE AND REAP THE BENEFITS

When you walk into a loan office with your debt paid down, a solid down payment in hand, your financial information organized, and prepared to put an automatic biweekly payment plan into action as soon as you close, you're ready to enjoy the full wealth-building benefits of homeownership. Get started today; that step alone will pay for your investment in this book thousands of times over.

KEY POINTS TO REMEMBER FROM THIS CHAPTER

- To be an Automatic Millionaire, you must own your home and pay it off early.
- There are many government agencies and companies that can help you buy a home with very little down.
- Getting the right mortgage and the right rate is the key to success.
- Paying off your mortgage early will save you tens or hundreds of thousands of dollars.
- Get your FICO score in shape before you shop for a loan to get the best rates.

EXERCISE
The Automatic Debt-Free Homeownership Motivator

How to use it: You know what to do: Write down action steps for the next 24 hours and 7 days and get moving on the path to becoming your own landlord.

THE AUTOMATIC DEBT-FREE HOMEOWNERSHIP MOTIVATOR

What is your biggest breakthrough from this chapter?

1

2

3

What are the most important actions you want to take in the next 24 hours?

1

2

3

What are the most important actions you want to take in the next 7 days?

1

2

3

What from this chapter do you want to share with someone else in your life?	Why?
1	
2	
3	

When you've finished the exercise: You've broken the mortgage lender code and learned how they make so much money off people who take 30 years to pay off their mortgages. Now you're ready to turn the tables, pay off your home early, and get rich faster!

Do you realize you have almost all the secrets to a lifetime of worry-free finances and future prosperity right in your hands, ready to put into action? That's amazing. Now let's look at how to clear the final obstacle that keeps many people from really getting rich: the deadly trap of credit card debt.

CHAPTER SEVEN

THE AUTOMATIC DEBT-FREE LIFESTYLE

Debt is a killer. Debt is the one thing that can cancel out all the great work you've done so far—learning your Latte Factor, Paying Yourself First, Making It Automatic, and so on. Debt forces us to work longer than we want to, taxes our savings, and often keeps us from reaching our goals.

What puts us in debt often are bad habits: running up big balances on our credit cards and then paying them down slowly—if at all. You have two choices: be held back by debt-causing habits, or take action to break them. Just as Jim and Sue McIntyre said at the beginning of this book, Automatic Millionaires don't do debt.

Through the ideas and exercises in this chapter, you're going to learn a series of concrete steps you can take to regain control over your credit cards and stay out of debt in the future. And if you don't have any credit card debt (congratulations!), what you read will motivate you to stay debt-free in the future.

BORROW MONEY TO MAKE MONEY, NOT LOSE IT

If you know anyone who lived through the Great Depression, you've heard their stories of total poverty. There were no jobs. People had no money.

Credit cards as we know them didn't exist. What that meant was, if you had no cash, you were in trouble. People who lived through the Depression came out of it with an intense dislike for debt and a deep belief in the importance of saving. Ask any Depression survivor about debt and I'll bet you get the same kind of answer: The only time borrowing makes sense is when you buy something that goes up in value, like a home.

EXERCISE
The "Gain Value or Lose Value" Checklist

Are the things you borrowed to buy gaining value or losing value?

How to use it: Write down your most expensive purchases and what you paid for them; then, in the last column, write down whether you think each purchase is going up or down in value. The real question to ask is "Am I buying an asset?" A pretty good guideline to follow is that the only possessions that consistently gain value are real estate, well-chosen stocks, art, collectibles, etc. Things like cars, clothing, computers, and electronics almost always lose value —unless they hang around long enough to become collectibles.

THE "GAIN VALUE OR LOSE VALUE" CHECKLIST			
What you bought	**What you paid**	**Your rate, if financing**	**Gaining/losing value?**
Example: *Motorcycle*	$18,750	8.5%	*Losing*

When you've finished the exercise: The point isn't to ask you to figure out how much your possessions are depreciating. That's grunt work that even accountants don't like. All I want you to do is become aware of how much of your debt is working *for* you and how much is working *against* you. Remember how I said that rich people make their money work for them? Well, going into debt for things that increase in value is an example of that. But piling up debt for things that only lose value is a sure ticket to a lifetime of financial woe.

TOO MANY AMERICANS ARE BIG HAT, NO CATTLE

Texans have a great way of describing someone trying to look like more than he really is. They say he's "big hat, no cattle." In other words, he might drive a fancy car and wear a ten-gallon hat, but he's no rancher. In fact, chances are there's probably no ranch.

I meet people like that every day. You probably do, too. They look rich. They have great cars, nice clothes, expensive watches, and all that. But when you look beneath the surface at their finances, you find that everything is rented or paid for with plastic. They don't really own anything. The banks own it. All they have is a mountain of credit card debt. *This is called leasing a lifestyle, not owning it.*

Too many Americans are wearing big hats made of debt. Together, Americans owe about half a *trillion* dollars in credit card debt. That's $8,400 per household. And the number is only rising.

AN AUTOMATIC MILLIONAIRE SUCCESS STORY

I have now read three of your books, *The Automatic Millionaire*, *Smart Women Finish Rich*, and *The Finish Rich Workbook*. I have learned so much. I have added to my mutual funds, started a simple IRA, added disability insurance and am applying for more life insurance because of your book. I have been teaching my step-children how easy it is to save a hundred dollars a month. I have started a retirement account for my 8-year-old daughter and also started a 529 account for her college. I am a 42-year-old hairstylist and I feel like I will actually be able to retire comfortably in 20 years. Thanks so much for writing these books—I've been telling all of my clients about them as well.

Karen MacKenzie

Eliot, ME

BRAINSTORMING BREAK

When did you get your first credit card? How did you use it?

WHY MOST AMERICANS WILL BE PAYING OFF THEIR CREDIT CARDS FOR THE REST OF THEIR LIVES

What do you think most people do when their credit card bill arrives in the mail every month? If you said, "Pay the minimum," you're right.

Let's say you're carrying that $8,400 average American debt on your credit card. If you pay the minimum amount every month on a card that charges 18% interest, how much do you think it will end up costing you?

Try **$20,615**. That's right. But wait—it's actually worse than that. It will take you 365 monthly payments to get your balance to zero—and that's assuming you never charge another dime on that card, never get hit with a late fee, and never pay an annual service fee. Imagine that—you would be paying off your credit card for more than 30 YEARS! You could buy and pay off a home in less time than that!

Here's the hard truth: You will never become an Automatic Millionaire if you run up credit card balances and pay only the minimum. Fortunately, that's not what you're going to do. I'm going to show you a better way.

EXERCISE
The Great Credit Flood Watch

This exercise is simple but very revealing. One of the biggest problems today for Americans trying to stay out of debt is that they're constantly tempted by credit card offers coming in the mail and offers of "easy credit terms" at retailers. To get an idea of how crazy things really are, I want you to see how much available credit is flooding into your life.

How to use it: Just write down all the credit offers you receive during one week: in the mail, from store clerks, over the phone—everything. Under "source," write where the offer came from and the company. Under "date," write down when you got the offer. Under "amount," write down the credit limit you were offered or the amount of the purchase you were told you could finance (such as a sofa for $2,500). Then, at the end of the week, add up the total number of credit solicitations you got and what they would have been worth.

THE GREAT CREDIT FLOOD WATCH

Week_____

CREDIT OFFERS RECEIVED

Source	Date	Amount

Total number of credit offers received this week: _____

Total dollar value of the credit offers: $_____

When you've finished the exercise: If you received less than a few credit solicitations of some kind, I'll be very surprised. But here's what you can do to stop receiving as many, at least in the mail: Go to **www.dmaconsumers. org**, click on the banner that says, "Remove my name from those lists," and then click on "How to remove your name from mailing lists." You'll find a form you can mail to the Direct Marketing Association for free (you can do the same thing online, but it costs you $5) and have your name taken off many of the direct-mail lists. It won't stop your junk mail and credit card offers, but it will slow the flood.

JUST SAY NO

One of the reasons why Americans are drowning in credit card debt is that credit is so incredibly easy to get. There are billions of dollars in credit lines being offered to us every day through the mail, at the mall, and by other means. So the first thing you're going to need to do is practice saying "No" to every credit offer that comes your way:

- **NO** to new credit cards
- **NO** to offers to transfer your balance
- **NO** to department store credit cards that offer one-time discounts
- **NO** to financing a big-ticket purchase like a big-screen TV or appliance, even if it comes with "no payments until 2010"
- **NO!** Repeat after me and keep saying it.

EXERCISE
How Much Do You Owe?

Do you have credit card debt? If you do, don't feel bad—you're hardly alone. The only thing that should make you feel bad is letting credit card debt keep you from becoming an Automatic Millionaire and reaching your goals. The first step is knowing exactly how much credit card debt you're carrying.

How to use it: Fill the blanks with your credit card debt information. For the last step, go to **www.finishrich.com**, click on "Start Here," "Free Resources," "Calculators—The Best of the Best," and then on "What will it take to pay off your credit card?" There you can find out how long it will take with the payments you're making now, and what you'd have to pay to retire your debt by a specific deadline.

HOW MUCH DO YOU OWE?

a. I have _____ credit cards in my name.

b. My spouse/partner has _____ credit cards in his/her name.

c. My children or other dependents have _____ credit cards in their names.

d. The combined outstanding balance owed on all these credit cards is $_____.

e. The average interest rate we're paying on these balances is _____ %.

f. The average amount we pay each month on all these cards is $_____.
   Now, go to **www.finishrich.com**, click on "Resources," "Calculators—The Best of the Best," and then on "What will it take to pay off your credit card?" Enter your numbers and enter them below.

g. With my current interest rates and payments, it will take _____ to bring the balances of all my credit cards down to $0.

When you've finished the exercise: Were you shocked by how long you could take to pay off your credit cards, assuming you never used them again? Most people are. Credit card debt creeps up on you; that's what makes it so dangerous. But now that you're aware of the dangers, you'll never be surprised again. The ones who *will* be surprised are the credit card companies . . . when you pay off your debt and cancel their cards!

AN AUTOMATIC MILLIONAIRE SUCCESS STORY

Thanks for writing such an awesome book! I've read my copy several times over and am heartened each time I realize that I've been taking the steps to become an Automatic Millionaire all along. I have increased my RRSP contributions to 10% of my gross pay. I take advantage of my mortgage options and increase my biweekly payments by 20% every calendar year. Right now, 71% of my mortgage payment goes to principal and 29% goes to interest. I set aside $100 each payday for my emergency fund. My student loans are gone and I have no credit card debt. The goal this year is to pay off my car loan and then reward myself with a trip to Hawaii next winter. I'm on the automatic plan to become a millionaire sooner rather than later and I just wanted to say thank you for showing me that I'm on the right path.

Camille Audain
Alberta, Canada

BEWARE OF THE CREDIT "QUICK FIX"

It's important to be realistic about credit card debt. You're not going to solve your problems overnight. After all, it probably took a long time to get into debt, so it stands to reason it will take a while to get out.

So I'd suggest looking at the so-called credit experts who claim they can solve your problems instantly with a healthy dose of skepticism. There are some "credit repair" companies out there that claim to be nonprofits but just charge you a big fee for services that aren't very valuable.

One reputable firm that you can trust is Consumer Credit Counseling Services. CCCS is an offshoot of the National Foundation for Credit Counseling, the nation's oldest national nonprofit organization for consumer counseling and education on budgeting, credit, and debt resolution. It has more than 1,300 local affiliates, and you can find one by going to **www.nfcc.org** or by calling 800-388-2777.

When you contact CCCS, they will refer you to a nonprofit credit-counseling group in your area. When you meet with this group, ask lots of questions about how they can help you. One of the most important questions is whether using their services will hurt your credit rating.

Before you sign on with any credit-repair group, find out what their fees are and check with the local chapter of the Better Business Bureau to see if they have any complaints lodged against them.

OPERATION "NO MORE DEBT": A FIVE-STEP PLAN FOR GETTING OUT OF DEBT AND STAYING OUT

STEP ONE: STOP DIGGING

If you're in a credit card hole and want to climb out, the first thing you need to do is quit making the hole deeper. That means you must stop digging. In other words, get rid of your credit cards. After all, you'd have to agree that a person who wants to get out of credit card debt but carries credit cards in his wallet is like an alcoholic who wants to quit drinking but carries a bottle of vodka in his car.

I speak from experience. I used to have a huge problem with credit card debt. When I was in college, I racked up over $10,000 in debt buying clothing, furniture, and other things I didn't need. I finally figured out that the only way to get out of debt was to STOP GOING SHOPPING WITH CREDIT CARDS IN MY POCKET.

EXERCISE
The Idle Credit Account Retirement Plan

Carrying five or six credit cards is a trap that encourages you to build up credit card debt. When one card is at its limit, you just pull out another! Well, as part of your journey toward being debt-free, you're going to close credit accounts you're not using. If you have a zero balance on some of your credit cards but you're keeping them "just in case," shut them down and cut them up! That's a great way to make progress toward being debt-free.

How to use it: You'll need your credit report to complete this exercise. When you have it, look down the list and find any credit cards you're not using (even if you cut the cards in half, if you didn't close the account, it's still open), along with any other open credit accounts you might have opened (for something like financing a piece of furniture, for example). Fill in the columns with the information you have, then start making calls to shut the accounts down. Record whom you talk to and what was said. When you confirm that an account has been closed, go back and check it off in the last column. It will feel great.

THE IDLE CREDIT ACCOUNT RETIREMENT PLAN					
Company	Type of account	Contact info	Whom I spoke to	What was said	Closed?

When you've finished the exercise: Your idle credit accounts are history . . . literally. Make sure you check your credit report again in three months to confirm that the accounts were indeed closed.

IMPORTANT NOTE

When closing idle credit accounts, it's not advisable to close ALL of your accounts at once, especially if you are planning to apply for a loan. Closing all your old accounts at once can lower your credit score and affect your ability to get a loan. The most important credit accounts to leave open are the OLDEST ones, because they show that you have an established credit history. However, leaving many credit accounts open can make you vulnerable to identity theft. So if you have multiple idle accounts, I suggest starting by closing the newest accounts first.

STEP TWO: RE-NEGOTIATE YOUR INTEREST RATES

Once you've taken steps to keep things from getting worse, now you can start to make things better. The best way to do that is to get your credit card company to lower the interest rate it charges you.

This is worth your time. Credit card interest rates have a huge impact on how much you have to pay and how long you're in debt. For example, let's say you have a card with a $2,000 balance at 18%. If you paid just the minimum, it would take you 222 months (that's 18½ years!) to pay the debt down to zero, and you'd pay $2,615.43 in interest. Ouch.

But if you got your rate cut to 9% and paid just the minimum, it would take you only 139 months (still over 12½ years, but better) to pay off the account, and you'd pay only $762.09 in interest. The interest rate makes a huge difference. Do your own calculations at **www.bankrate.com.**

There are three steps to lowering your credit card rates. I'll explain them, and then you can use the worksheet that follows to actually go through the process and get your interest rates lowered. Let's get started.

1. **Find out how much interest you're paying now.** Read the fine print on your credit card statement. It should tell you your APR, or Annualized Percentage Rate. That's how much you're paying per year on your debt. If your statement is confusing (and many are; after all, the bank doesn't really want you to know how badly it's ripping you off), call your credit card company. Ask them for your *annual* rate, NOT the "rate above prime."

2. **Ask for a lower rate.** This is surprisingly effective. After all, you have leverage—credit card companies make money off you, so they want to keep your business. If your current interest rate is too high, tell the credit card company you'd like them to lower it. If they say no, tell them you'll be closing your account this week and transferring your balance to a competitor who offers better rates. So they know you're serious, name the competitor (this should be easy; just look at your Credit Flood worksheet). Most companies will drop your rate then and there to keep from losing you. But if you really want a good rate, ask to talk

to a supervisor, then ask to have your rate cut in half. Supervisors have the authority to cut your rate right over the phone. You can even get them to waive your annual fee.

3. **Consolidate your debt.** Now that you're feeling powerful after twisting the arms of your credit card companies, it's time to really take control by consolidating all your credit card balances on one low-rate card. This is another situation where you should "just ask." When you're negotiating with credit card companies for a lower rate, tell them that you're prepared to move all your balances to the company that offers you the lowest rate. To find out what "low" is, go to **www.bankrate.com** or the business section of your newspaper and find out the current credit card rates. I suggest finding out what the national average is—and asking for half that rate. Even better, ask the credit card company what it's willing to offer customers like you who are willing to consolidate their debt. Let them sell you! You might get six months of no interest or something else equally appealing. Be careful, though: Make sure there are no catches. For example, six months interest-free might be followed by a rate that jumps to 25% in the seventh month. Always ask questions and never assume. The object here is not to jump from one low rate to another, but to find the lowest rate, then follow Steps 4 and 5 to get out of debt completely, forever.

EXERCISE
The Great Rate Re-negotiator

How to use it: Use this worksheet to keep a clear record of all the rate negotiations you have with credit card companies. In the top half, write down the information about your conversations with your credit card companies when you asked them to lower your rate. In the lower half, write down what you were told when you called competing companies about transferring your balances to their cards. In the last column, once you've made your calls, mark down which companies are getting your business and which are losing it. And at the bottom, once you're done with all your calls and all your decisions, record your new interest rates and new credit card companies—if anyone was foolish enough to lose your business.

THE GREAT RATE RE-NEGOTIATOR

MY CURRENT CREDIT CARD COMPANIES

Company	Balance	Current rate	Spoke to:	Offer	Staying/ Going?

NEW COMPANIES I'VE CALLED

Company	What they offered	Accepting/Declining?

MY CREDIT CARDS AND RATES GOING FORWARD

Credit card # 1

Old company _____   New company _____

Old rate _____ %   New rate _____ %

Credit card # 2

Old company _____   New company _____

Old rate _____ %   New rate _____ %

Credit card # 3

Old company _____   New company _____

Old rate _____ %   New rate _____ %

Credit card # 4

Old company _____   New company _____

Old rate _____ %   New rate _____ %

When you've finished the exercise: Look at those lower rates. Savor them. Enjoy the sweet smell of victory . . . at least for now. You've taken a huge step toward getting out of debt. You've also showed the credit card companies who's boss, and that always feels great!

STEP THREE: BURY THE PAST, JUMP TO THE FUTURE

Earlier, we saw how the kind of wealth you will build is determined by the way cash flows through your life. With that in mind, I suggested that you set a goal of Paying Yourself First at least 10% of your pretax income. But if you're in credit card debt, you need a different plan.

Here it is: Whatever amount you decide to Pay Yourself First, split it in half. Put 50% in your retirement account and use 50% to pay off your debt. Once the debt is paid, you can revert to Paying Yourself First with the full 100%.

If you make $50,000 a year, Paying Yourself First 10% would mean setting aside $5,000 a year, or $416 a month. But if you have credit card debt, you'd split that in half, putting aside $208 a month and using the other $208 to pay off credit cards.

This system lets you feel like you're working for the future while erasing the mistakes of the past. So the rationale is as much emotional as financial.

I call this my "Bury the Past, Jump to the Future" system. Try it. It really works.

EXERCISE
The Pay Yourself First 50% Debt Paydown

How to use it: Fill in the blanks to figure out how much money you can put toward your debt every month while still Paying Yourself First.

THE PAY YOURSELF FIRST 50% DEBT PAYDOWN

a. Gross annual income _____

b. Pay Yourself First amount (10% of gross) _____

c. Amount for retirement savings (b ÷ 2) _____

d. Amount for paying off credit card debt (b ÷ 2) _____

Amount I will pay on my credit card(s) each month (d ÷ 12): $ _____

When you've finished the exercise: Now start making those payments and watching your balances fall! If you have more than one card and you're not sure which to pay first, I've given you the answer in the very next section.

STEP FOUR: DOLP™ YOUR DEBT OUT OF EXISTENCE

What if, for some reason (for example, you owe so much that no company will give you a sufficient credit limit), you can't consolidate your debts on one credit card? There's another way to get out of credit card debt systematically: DOLP your way out of debt.

DOLP stands for Dead On Last Payment. What that means is that you're going to pay off your credit cards one at a time, and the minute you get each one paid off, you're going to close that account. One more dead debt.

Of course, when you have a lot of credit cards, it can be pretty confusing to figure out how to pay them off. Should you pay a little on all of them? Or should you concentrate on one card at a time? If so, which card do you pay off first?

This is where the DOLP system comes in. Here's what you do:

1. Make a list of the current outstanding balances on each of your credit cards.
2. Divide each balance by the minimum payment that particular card company wants from you. That's that account's DOLP number. For example, your outstanding balance with one Visa account is $500 and the

minimum payment due is $50. Divide $500 by $50 and you get a DOLP number of 10.

3. Once you've figured out the DOLP number for each account, rank them in reverse order, putting the account with the lowest DOLP number first. The resulting table should look like this:

Account	Outstanding Balance	Minimum Monthly Payment	DOLP Number (balance ÷ minimum payment)	DOLP Ranking
Visa	$500	$50	10	1
MasterCard	$775	$65	12	2
AMEX	$1,150	$35	39	3

ONCE YOU KNOW IT, PAY 'EM OFF!

Now you know the most efficient order for paying off your various credit card balances—pay off the card with the lowest DOLP ranking *first*. As you can see, instead of paying a small amount on all your cards, my emphasis is on getting one card paid off and the account closed as soon as possible. The more debt you retire, the more money you'll have to pay off your larger balances.

> ### AN AUTOMATIC MILLIONAIRE SUCCESS STORY
>
> I bought your book after seeing you on *The Oprah Winfrey Show*. The first thing I did was call my credit card company and ask for a rate decrease. I let them know that I had compared rates on bankrate.com and they decreased my APR by more than HALF!!! I am plowing through the rest of my to-dos now and can't wait to get them all rolling. Thank you for giving this great information to everyone!
>
> **Jane Reede**
> **Santa Clara, CA**

So take half your Pay Yourself First money and apply it to the card with the lowest DOLP ranking (your Visa in this example). For all the others, make the minimum payment. Once you've DOLPed that account, close it immediately. Then take that Pay Yourself First money and start putting it toward the credit card with the next-lowest DOLP ranking. Continue doing this until you're debt-free.

Here's a blank DOLP table you can use for your accounts:

Account	Outstanding Balance	Minimum Monthly Payment	DOLP Number (balance ÷ minimum payment)	DOLP Ranking

STEP FIVE: NOW MAKE IT AUTOMATIC!

You knew we'd come back to this, didn't you? The key to your entire financial future is making all these smart steps automatic—and that includes paying off your debt. Fortunately, setting up an automatic payment plan for your credit card debt is easy. Just call your credit card holder and tell them you'd like to arrange for them to make an automatic debit from your checking account each month. If they can't, call your bank and sign up for a free online bill-paying service (most banks have it these days) that allows you to have money automatically transferred from your checking account to your credit card company on a specific date each month. Then calculate your Pay Yourself First amount, cut it in half, and you're in business!

BRAINSTORMING BREAK

What will your strategy be for using credit cards from now on?

Can you believe this? We're almost done . . . and you've made unbelievable progress. Right now, today, you've learned more than 90% of the people in this country know about money, just by the things you've done as you've read this workbook. But before we finish, it's time to take the final step and look at how to make the world—and your life—better with automatic tithing.

KEY POINTS TO REMEMBER FROM THIS CHAPTER

- Never borrow money unless you can use it to make more money.
- Just say "No" to all future credit offers.
- Re-negotiating your credit card interest rates can save you thousands. If card holders won't lower your rate, transfer your balances to others who will.
- DOLP your debt out of existence.

EXERCISE
The Automatic Debt-Free Lifestyle Motivator

How to use it: You're a master at this now, I'm sure. You know what you need to do: Write down the key steps you're going to take in the next 24 hours and 7 days toward getting rid of that ugly, nasty credit card debt forever.

THE AUTOMATIC DEBT-FREE LIFESTYLE MOTIVATOR

What is your biggest breakthrough from this chapter?

1

2

3

What are the most important actions you want to take in the next 24 hours?

1

2

3

What are the most important actions you want to take in the next 7 days?

1

2

3

What from this chapter do you want to share with someone else in your life?	Why?
1	
2	
3	

When you've finished the exercise: If I gave out advanced degrees in becoming an Automatic Millionaire, you'd have your master's. You're almost done, and you've learned so much that's already changing your financial future. Even if you haven't implemented your plan yet, you've changed your future . . . because you'll never think of debt the same way again.

Now let's finish our journey by looking at the last part of being a true Automatic Millionaire: *making your life and the world better by giving back.*

CHAPTER EIGHT

MAKE A DIFFERENCE WITH AUTOMATIC TITHING

We make a living by what we earn—we make a life by what we give.
—Winston Churchill

Having bought this book and read it all the way through to the final chapter makes you very special. Congratulations. I hope you have been inspired to take some simple actions that will dramatically impact your life.

What you've read in this book are tried-and-true strategies for building wealth and financial security automatically. Put them into action and you will achieve your dreams. But if you focus only on the result, you're missing half the fun: the journey. Becoming an Automatic Millionaire is also about relieving stress and enjoying your life. In other words, it's not just about securing your future but about making your present wonderful.

With that in mind, I'd like to share one last step in our journey together—one that enables you to feel like a millionaire even if it's years before you become one. How? By using the tools you've already learned to become a giver . . . to make the world a better place.

THERE'S MORE TO LIFE THAN MONEY

The idea that there's more to life than money may seem strange to read in a book about how to become a millionaire. But it's true. Deep down, we all know it.

Don't get me wrong. Money is good. I sincerely hope you get all the riches you want. As the saying goes, I've seen rich and I've seen poor, and rich is better. But there's one thing money absolutely cannot do, and that's give your life meaning.

Why do we pursue wealth? I think it's for much more than the things money can buy—it's for the *feeling* those things give us. The fancy car, the expensive home—what we really savor are the feelings those things inspire in us. And though you may be years from actually being rich, you can enjoy the *feeling* of being wealthy in a matter of days.

Want me to tell you how?

EXERCISE
The Tithing Scorecard

How to use it: This is an easy one. Just list the organizations or causes that you donate to right now, how much you give each year on average, and how long you've been giving. In the last column, explain why you choose to give to each cause. Then, at the bottom, total up how much you give in a typical year.

THE TITHING SCORECARD			
Charity	**Average annual gift**	**How long?**	**Why?**
Humane Society	*$200*	*5 years*	*Because I love animals*
CURRENT ANNUAL GIVING: $ _____			

When you've finished the exercise: See how generous you are? Many Americans don't even know how much they give to worthy causes during the year, because the giving happens a little at a time. Automatic tithing will change all that. You'll know exactly how much you give—and if it's enough to make you feel that you're making a difference.

HAVING IT ALL THROUGH TITHING

Tithing has been around nearly as long as civilization. It's a tradition in many cultures—a person who has been blessed with abundance should set aside a portion of what he or she receives to help others who don't have as much. The gifts can be money, time, compassion, or even ideas. But what's really amazing is that when you tithe, you get a feeling that simply acquiring material things can't provide. You feel wonderful.

You see, that's the great lie of consumer culture: the idea that getting more things will make you feel better. That's why we spend so much and get into so much debt—to get the high that comes with acquiring the new car or the new watch. But it doesn't work. The high fades and we're left feeling empty and disappointed.

One of the best things about tithing is that the feeling doesn't fade. It feels great because you're doing something real. You're helping others. Trust me, if you take this last step and begin tithing automatically, you'll never listen to the consumer lie again. You'll have found something much, much better.

AN AUTOMATIC MILLIONAIRE SUCCESS STORY

As did my father, I enjoyed *The Automatic Millionaire*. Just like my father, I plan to never have a credit card; a debit card is just fine.

I was home schooled and began working for a salary as a grader in a private school at age fourteen. My father taught me the value of saving. I am now eighteen and meet all the requirements of becoming a millionaire. That is without adding another penny. I started my IRA at fourteen and my stock account as well.

Thank you for the book—it reinforces what I already knew from believing in my father.

Shannon McGinnis
Tarboro, NC

TITHING GIVES BACK MORE
THAN YOU GIVE AWAY

You've probably heard of the concept of tithing, perhaps in the context of your church, temple, or mosque. The word is based on the Old Anglo-Saxon word for "tenth," and the original idea was that you were supposed to donate to charity 10% of what you harvested from the land each year. But tithing has changed. It's no longer about following tradition or getting rid of guilt or making yourself look good. It's about the pure joy of giving.

But here's the amazing thing, and it's probably the answer to your question "What's this stuff about giving doing in a book about getting rich?" Though giving should always be for its own sake, the truth is that abundance tends to flow back to those who give. The more you give, the more comes back to you: more love, more joy, more opportunity, more wealth, more relationships, more meaning in your life.

If you think about it, it makes perfect sense. Wealth doesn't inspire anybody; generosity of spirit does. By giving, you attract people into your orbit, people who may bring not only financial or business opportunity but wisdom, friendship, or a shared passion. Money and all the best things in life really do flow faster to those who give. Givers attract abundance.

BRAINSTORMING BREAK

What changes would you like to help bring about in your community?

EXERCISE
Which Charities Fit Your Values?

Now that you've thought about the changes you'd like to see happen, give some thought to which organizations in your community are trying to address those concerns. Which organizations match your values?

How to use this exercise: List charitable or activist organizations you are curious about, along with their web addresses. Once you check out their web sites and ask around among people you know who have worked with these groups, write down the ways in which they appeal to you and the ways they don't fit your vision. Finally, check off the organizations you will look into working with in the future.

WHICH CHARITIES FIT YOUR VALUES?			
Name of organization and web address	**Things I like about them**	**Things I don't like**	**I'll look further** ✓

When you've finished the exercise: You'll have a better road map for charities that suit your values and can make better decisions about tithing and volunteering your time and energy.

HOW TO TITHE

Should you tithe? It's a personal decision, of course. But if you're not doing it now, I'd like to suggest that you try. Take a percentage of your income and start donating it to one or more worthy causes. You could donate the 10% traditionally associated with tithing, or more, or less. Give whatever you're comfortable with. It's not about how much you give but about the love of giving. The most important thing is getting started.

I suggest starting small—say with 1% of your income—and letting your contributions grow over time, just as you're doing with Pay Yourself First. Not only will that create momentum that will change your life, but you'll also be helping others.

If this sounds good to you, take a look at the simple Five-Step Tithing Plan that follows. If you're in a relationship, talk about it with your partner. If it feels right, try it. You'll be amazed at how much doing things for others can do for you.

STEP ONE: COMMIT TO TITHING

Tithing needs to be a consistent commitment, just like Pay Yourself First. If you donate a set percentage of your income every time you get paid, you'll end the year with an impressive contribution record. If you wait until the end of the year to donate "what's left," it's likely you won't give anything.

I'm not suggesting for a moment that you go into debt to tithe—not after you've worked so hard to pay off your credit card balances. Instead, select a percentage of your income that feels comfortable to you, then commit to donating that percentage every month. Think of it as your way of helping to change the world.

STEP TWO: NOW MAKE IT AUTOMATIC!

You saw this coming, didn't you? Just as with all the other steps in becoming an Automatic Millionaire, automating your tithing is the key to success. Whatever amount you decide to tithe, arrange to have it automatically deducted from your checking account on the same day every month. Most organized charities will help you arrange an automatic transfer schedule, so this should be easy. If you're not comfortable with this, it should be simple enough to set up an automatic transfer through your bank.

STEP THREE: RESEARCH THE CHARITY BEFORE YOU GIVE

Where you donate your money is a personal decision. The most important advice I can offer is that you make sure the charity to which you give your hard-earned dollars is really using them to help the people or causes it's supposed to be helping. Charities are big businesses, and in some of them a big chunk of the contributions they receive end up going to pay for salaries and administrative costs. I'd suggest avoiding those organizations.

I speak from experience. I once got involved with a charitable cause that was important to me, and I donated a week of my time to raise $20,000 in contributions, which felt really good. Then I found out that less than 40% of the money the organization received was going to the cause. I was very disappointed.

It is very rare for a charity to pass through 100% of the donations it gets. There are always expenses to pay. But experts recommend looking for charitable organizations that pass through at least 75% and staying away from those that pass through less than 50%.

Before you become a generous giver, become a smart giver. These are some of the best online resources I've found for learning more about charitable organizations:

CHARITY RESEARCH RESOURCES	
www.justgive.org	This user-friendly web site is a great place to start, with links to and information about more than 850,000 charitable organizations.
www.give.org	The web site of the BBB Wise Giving Alliance, a nonprofit clearinghouse formed in 2001 to distribute information on nonprofits that solicit donations nationally or have national or international program services. See what they have to say about any organization you're considering donating to.
www.guidestar.org	Guidestar aims to make charitable giving easy by doing the kind of due diligence that philanthropists don't always have time for. Its site is loaded with helpful data.
www.irs.gov	Before you donate money to any organization, find out if it's recognized by the IRS as a bona fide tax-exempt organization under section 501(c)(3) of the tax code. The IRS site has a wealth of information about giving to charitable groups.

EXERCISE
The Charity Research Report

How to use it: Write down the names of charitable organizations that you might want to give to. Then go to the charity research web sites I've listed for you to learn more about each one. On this worksheet, list the organization, the cause it's involved in, and contact information and names. Then start by asking the four questions I've given you and writing down the answers. Ask any additional questions that might occur to you as well.

Finally, when you've decided that a charity is worth your time and money, check it off.

THE CHARITY RESEARCH REPORT

Organization: **Cause:**

Contact Information: **Contact Person:**

QUESTIONS

1. Is my contribution tax-deductible?

2. What % of donated funds go to your administrative costs?

3. Will you send me a year-end record of my total donations?

4. Can I donate via an automatic transfer from my bank account?

I will make this organization part of my Tithing Plan   _____ YES   _____ NO

Organization: **Cause:**

Contact Information: **Contact Person:**

QUESTIONS

1. Is my contribution tax-deductible?

2. What % of donated funds go to your administrative costs?

3. Will you send me a year-end record of my total donations?

4. Can I donate via an automatic transfer from my bank account?

I will make this organization part of my Tithing Plan   _____ YES   _____ NO

Organization: **Cause:**

Contact Information: **Contact Person:**

QUESTIONS

1. Is my contribution tax-deductible?

2. What % of donated funds go to your administrative costs?

3. Will you send me a year-end record of my total donations?

4. Can I donate via an automatic transfer from my bank account?

I will make this organization part of my Tithing Plan   _____ YES   _____ NO

Organization: **Cause:**

Contact Information: **Contact Person:**

QUESTIONS

1. Is my contribution tax-deductible?

2. What % of donated funds go to your administrative costs?

3. Will you send me a year-end record of my total donations?

4. Can I donate via an automatic transfer from my bank account?

I will make this organization part of my Tithing Plan   _____ YES   _____ NO

When you've finished the exercise: Now you have two lists—organizations you're giving to today, and ones you might want to give to tomorrow. From these you can create a master list of charities, which is exactly what we're going to do in a little while.

STEP FOUR: KEEP TRACK OF YOUR DEDUCTIBLE CONTRIBUTIONS

To encourage Americans to give, the U.S. government has long allowed taxpayers to deduct contributions to qualified charities. Depending on how much you give, you can offset as much as 50% of your income this way.

Just because an organization calls itself a charity doesn't mean donations to it are tax-deductible. For donations to be deductible, the organization must apply for tax-exempt status under section 501(c)(3) of the tax code.

You should always keep track of your charitable donations. For contributions of less than $250, the IRS requires you to keep some sort of written record, such as a canceled check, a receipt from the recipient, or a credit card statement. If you give more than $250, you must file proof of your donation with your tax returns.

AN AUTOMATIC MILLIONAIRE SUCCESS STORY

I am the sole breadwinner raising four kids. By the time I read through Chapter Six in *The Automatic Millionaire* on buying a house, I was fed up thinking I could never save 10%, while building 6 months' emergency cash, while paying off my debts, and saving to purchase a house. But it was the last chapter of the book, on tithing, that inspired me. I finished the book on Sunday, and on Monday I started putting 5% gross into my 401(k) plan at work. Since the company matches 50% of my contributions up to 5% gross, I am effectively saving 7.5% of my gross pay. I'll have to pack peanut butter and jelly all week (my Latte Factor was $20 wasted a week!) but my wife and I are on our way! Thank you for the inspiration and the motivation! You'll hear more and better things from me in the future. I—make that WE—just know it! God bless.

Don and Shirley Aydelotte
Fayetteville, NC

Be aware that not all charitable donations are 100% deductible. Say you spend $500 on tickets to a charity event where you play in a golf tournament or attend a dinner. Because you've received a benefit in return for your contribution, only a portion of your $500 will be deductible. The charity should be able to tell you how much.

EXERCISE
The Annual Charitable Giving Report

How to use it: You've done the research. Now is the time to choose the organizations you want to include in your automatic tithing plan.

Once you've chosen, make copies of this worksheet and use it each year to track exactly which charities you're donating to and how much you're giving. Just fill in the organization name, the amount you give per month, your total for the year, what percentage of the gift is tax-deductible, and if you've received written proof of your donation from the group. At the bottom, total your charitable giving for the year and the amount that's tax-deductible.

THE ANNUAL CHARITABLE GIVING REPORT				
Tax Year _____				
Charity	Monthly gift	Annual total	% Tax-deductible	Written proof?
Humane Society	*$50*	*$600*	*100%*	*yes*

TOTAL GIVING FOR THE YEAR: $ _____

AMOUNT THAT'S DEDUCTIBLE: $ _____

When you've finished the exercise: You're ready to automate your tithing plan and get started with your giving!

STEP FIVE: FIND OUT ABOUT DONOR-ADVISED MUTUAL FUNDS

In recent years, a new type of mutual fund investment has appeared: donor-advised or charity funds. Designed specifically for charity-minded investors, they allow people to invest their money for a charity's benefit later while enjoying a tax break now.

These funds offer a number of benefits:

- **Instant tax deduction.** Once your money is deposited into one of these funds, you can take a tax deduction based on your IRS limits the same year, even though the money may not go to a charity until a later date.
- **More money for charities.** One of the best features of these funds is that contributions grow tax-deferred like an IRA. And they offer a terrific tax advantage to people who want to donate securities that have substantially appreciated. For instance, say you bought a stock or mutual fund whose price has soared. Instead of selling it and paying a hefty capital gains tax, you can simply deposit the stock into a charity fund. You get your tax deduction immediately, and the investment grows tax-free until you direct the fund to cut a check to a selected charity.
- **Less pressure.** These funds are great for people who want to give but don't know what organizations they want to give to. You can let the money grow, get the deduction, and make up your mind about a worthy charity later.
- **Creation of a legacy.** As your wealth grows (and it will because of what you're doing), you'll begin to make a lasting difference in the world. Donor funds allow you to build a real charitable base for your family, since more than one person can contribute to the fund.

Keep in mind that once you invest in one of these funds, you've made an irrevocable gift. You can't get the money back. So it's critical that you make the right choice of fund. Here are three established donor funds worth considering:

TOP DONOR-ADVISED MUTUAL FUNDS			
Company	Phone Number	Web Site	Minimum Investment
Fidelity Charitable Gift Fund	800-682-4438	www.charitablegift.org	$10,000
Schwab Fund for Charitable Giving	800-746-6216	www.schwabcharitable.org	$10,000
The T. Rowe Price Program for Charitable Giving	800-564-1597	www.programforgiving.org	$10,000

SOME OF THE WORLD'S WEALTHIEST PEOPLE TITHED BEFORE THEY BECAME RICH

If you study the lives of the great leaders, visionaries, and businesspeople of our time, you will find a thread linking them: Long before they made their fortunes, they started giving.

A great example is Sir John Templeton. One of the world's greatest investors and a billionaire many times over, Templeton is recognized today as one of the world's great philanthropists. But he didn't wait for riches to start tithing. Back in the days when he and his wife were earning only $50 a week, they Paid Themselves First 50% of their income—and still managed to tithe. And he became a billionaire.

Something to think about?

BRAINSTORMING BREAK

How could tithing benefit you?

KEY POINTS TO REMEMBER FROM THIS CHAPTER

- Giving creates abundance in your life.
- Charitable giving can give you significant tax savings.
- There are many charities. Research before you give.
- Most reputable charities will allow you to contribute automatically.

EXERCISE
The Automatic Tithing Motivator

How to use it: You've got this down by now: Fill in your goals for the next 24 hours and 7 days and get started.

THE AUTOMATIC TITHING MOTIVATOR

What is your biggest breakthrough from this chapter?

1	
2	
3	

What are the most important actions you want to take in the next 24 hours?

1	
2	
3	

What are the most important actions you want to take in the next 7 days?

1	
2	
3	

What from this chapter do you want to share with someone else in your life?	Why?
1	
2	
3	

When you've finished the exercise: You're ready to automate the last piece in your Automatic Millionaire plan, which means you're ready to get the ball rolling, then sit back and enjoy the knowledge that every day, you're building a bright, secure future for yourself . . . and making the world a better place.

Congratulations! You're ready to become an Automatic Millionaire! I think a celebration is in order—you've just done more for your financial future in a few hours than most people do in their entire lives. I have a few more things to say, so if you'll flip to the next chapter, we'll look at your Power Charges, and then you'll be on your way to changing your life!

CHAPTER NINE

YOUR JOURNEY BEGINS TODAY!

You really have come a long way in this workbook. I'm proud of you for both reading this book and doing the exercises. Many people buy workbooks with great intentions, but then they don't do the work. It takes some work to be rich. You have to actually take action. But the secret to being an Automatic Millionaire is that you ideally take action once—by setting up your plan automatically. Then you are done and can go back to enjoying your life.

THE POWER CHARGE WORKSHEETS

It's important to realize what you've accomplished, so I've created a tool I call the POWER CHARGE™. The point of this tool is to remind yourself how far you've come in both your knowledge and your actions by reading *The Automatic Millionaire Workbook*. The Power Charge Worksheets are designed to be your Automatic Millionaire success journal—your way of keeping track of all the steps you take, chapter by chapter, to put your plan into action.

In the beginning of the book, I recommended that you use these tools to track the progress you've made, so it's possible that you've already completed them. The point of tracking your progress is to focus on what you've done right! All too often, especially when it comes to our money, we forget the steps forward we've taken, and we focus on what we haven't done. Focusing on what you haven't done can cripple your spirit, making it harder to take action to move forward. On the other hand, seeing how much you've already accomplished (like reading this book) can give you the confidence to take even more action toward your goals and dreams. So let's go over the Power Charge Worksheets, and if you haven't done any of them yet, consider taking a few minutes to jot down some of the positive progress you've made. I think you'll be impressed.

EXERCISE
Your Power Charges

How to use it: For each chapter of this workbook, you have a Power Charge. As you progress through the steps I've outlined in each chapter—opening an IRA, for example, in Pay Yourself First—write it down. In the first column, write down what you did. In the second, write down how this will help your future. In the third column, write down what your next action should be. Finally, write down the name of the person you will share your success with. Realistically, you won't share everything you've done, but you might share the big things. If you go from saving nothing to paying yourself 10% of your income, that's worth sharing with a friend. If you find your Latte Factor and it helps you start getting out of debt faster, that's worth sharing with someone you love. You might become the inspiration your family, coworker, or best friend needs to get their financial life on track.

Each time you take a step toward becoming an Automatic Millionaire, come back here and write it down! Even more important, look back on how far you've come!

MEETING THE AUTOMATIC MILLIONAIRE POWER CHARGE			
What I've Done	How This Will Help My Future	Next Actions to Take	Whom I'll Share My Success With

THE LATTE FACTOR POWER CHARGE			
What I've Done	**How This Will Help My Future**	**Next Actions to Take**	**Whom I'll Share My Success With**

PAY YOURSELF FIRST POWER CHARGE			
What I've Done	How This Will Help My Future	Next Actions to Take	Whom I'll Share My Success With

MAKE IT AUTOMATIC POWER CHARGE			
What I've Done	How This Will Help My Future	Next Actions to Take	Whom I'll Share My Success With

AUTOMATE FOR A RAINY DAY POWER CHARGE			
What I've Done	**How This Will Help My Future**	**Next Actions to Take**	**Whom I'll Share My Success With**

AUTOMATIC DEBT-FREE HOMEOWNERSHIP POWER CHARGE			
What I've Done	**How This Will Help My Future**	**Next Actions to Take**	**Whom I'll Share My Success With**

AUTOMATIC DEBT-FREE LIFESTYLE POWER CHARGE			
What I've Done	How This Will Help My Future	Next Actions to Take	Whom I'll Share My Success With

MAKE A DIFFERENCE WITH AUTOMATIC TITHING POWER CHARGE			
What I've Done	**How This Will Help My Future**	**Next Actions to Take**	**Whom I'll Share My Success With**

After you've finished the exercise: By the time you're done, you should be celebrating, because you'll be on your way to becoming an official Automatic Millionaire, well on your way to a worry-free life of security and fulfillment!

HOW DID YOU ANSWER
THE FIVE QUESTIONS?

Remember the Five Questions I told you I could ask that would tell me with 90% certainty if you would become a millionaire? Just to refresh your memory, they are:

1. Do you know your Latte Factor?
2. Do you "Pay Yourself First"?
3. Have you made your financial plan automatic?
4. Do you own your home?
5. Do you tithe?

When we talked about the Five Questions before, I didn't ask you to write down your answers. But now that you know what each of those questions really means, it's time to see where you stand. Remember that if you answer "Yes" to all five questions, you've got an excellent opportunity to become a millionaire. If you still haven't started yet, don't get depressed—just remember these questions and your goal to have a "yes" answer to them going forward.

EXERCISE
The Five Questions Checklist

How to use it: First, write down your answer for each of the Five Questions *today*. Forget about where you want to be; where are you now? Then give a brief explanation why your answer is what it is. In the third column, write down what you need to do to make your answer "Yes" if it isn't already. The final column is the exciting one: When you take the action that makes your answer "Yes," write down the date. It's a personal holiday!

THE FIVE QUESTIONS CHECKLIST			
1. Do you know your Latte Factor?			
Today's Answer	Explanation	Actions Needed	"Yes" Date
2. Do you Pay Yourself First?			
Today's Answer	Explanation	Actions Needed	"Yes" Date
3. Have you made your plan automatic?			
Today's Answer	Explanation	Actions Needed	"Yes" Date
4. Do you own your own home?			
Today's Answer	Explanation	Actions Needed	"Yes" Date
5. Do you tithe?			
Today's Answer	Explanation	Actions Needed	"Yes" Date

After you've finished the exercise: Get started on making all your answers "Yes!"

YOUR FUTURE IS BRIGHT

In the end, whichever part of *The Automatic Millionaire Workbook* inspired you most, there's one question you should ask yourself: "Why not?" Why not apply what you've learned? If the way you're managing your money right now isn't getting you the results you want, why not try something that's so simple and effective? If you don't like it, you can always go back to what you were doing.

But I'm betting you won't. You see, I know these simple steps work. I've seen them work for thousands of readers and people who have attended my seminars. And I predict that once you set the Automatic Millionaire system in motion, you'll never want to go back to the old way. Why?

Because instead of being stressed about retirement, you'll know you have a bright future ahead of you, where you can do anything you want with your later years . . .

Because instead of wasting money every day without thinking about it, you'll be putting that money to work for you . . .

Because instead of living "without a net" like so many Americans, you'll have money saved to keep you secure in case "life happens" . . .

Because instead of finding excuses not to contribute to your retirement accounts every month and then feeling guilty about it, you'll know that every month, your wealth is growing automatically . . .

Because instead of renting, you'll become a homeowner. And if you already own a home, instead of wasting a fortune on a 30-year mortgage, you'll pay your home off early . . .

Because you'll make the credit card companies hate you by paying off your balances, cutting your cards in half, and refusing all their new card offers . . .

Because you'll be enjoying greater prosperity and sharing some of it with others less fortunate than yourself . . .

Because you'll be on your way to becoming an Automatic Millionaire!

TAKE OTHERS ON THIS JOURNEY

My other hope is that as you realize how simple becoming an Automatic Millionaire is, you'll go a step further and teach your friends to become Automatic Millionaires, too, so they can join you on this journey.

Imagine your life 10 years from now, with no debt, money in the bank, a home with a ton of equity, and a plan in place that will enable you to become rich and give something back to help others. Now imagine how great that would be if those you loved were doing the same thing!

I know you are a special person with unique dreams and gifts. I know you deserve all the success in the world. I know you deserve to see your dreams come true. If you take only one thing away from this book, make it this: *You can do it.*

If this workbook has helped you, opened your eyes, made you focus and take steps toward your future wealth, I'd love to hear from you. Please share your successes, insights, discoveries, challenges, and stories by e-mailing them to me via our web site at **www.finishrich.com.** And until we meet again, enjoy your journey, and Live and Finish Rich.

ABOUT THE AUTHOR

David Bach has helped millions of people around the world take action to live and finish rich. He is the author of the #1 *New York Times* bestseller *The Automatic Millionaire* as well as the national bestsellers *Smart Women Finish Rich, Smart Couples Finish Rich,* and *The Finish Rich Workbook.* Bach carries the unique distinction of having all four books in his FinishRich Series appear *simultaneously* on the *Wall Street Journal, BusinessWeek,* and *USA Today* bestseller lists. He is also the author of *1001 Financial Words You Need to Know,* the first financial dictionary published by Oxford University Press. In all, his books have been published in ten languages with more than two million copies in print worldwide.

Regularly featured on television and radio as well as in newspapers and magazines, Bach has appeared twice on *The Oprah Winfrey Show to* share his strategies for living and finishing rich. He is also a regular contributor to CNN's *American Morning* and has appeared regularly on ABC's *The View,* NBC's *Today* and *Weekend Today* shows, CBS's *Early Show,* Fox News Channel's *The O'Reilly Factor,* CNBC's *Power Lunch,* CNNfn, and MSNBC. He has been profiled in numerous major publications, including the *New York Times, BusinessWeek, USA Today, People, Reader's Digest, Time, Financial Times,* the *Washington Post,* the *Wall Street Journal, Los Angeles Times, San Francisco Chronicle, Working Woman, Glamour,* and *Family Circle.*

David Bach is the creator of the FinishRich® seminar series, which highlights his quick and easy-to-follow financial strategies, from which millions have benefited. In just the last few years, more than half a million people have attended his Smart Women Finish Rich® and Smart Couples Finish Rich® seminars, which have been taught throughout North America by thousands of financial advisors in more than 2,000 cities. Each month, through these seminars, men and women learn firsthand how to take financial action to live a life in line with their values.

A renowned financial speaker, Bach regularly presents seminars for and delivers keynote addresses to the world's leading financial service firms,

Fortune 500 companies, universities, and national conferences. He is the founder and CEO of FinishRich, Inc., a company dedicated to revolutionizing the way people learn about money. Prior to founding FinishRich, Inc., he was a senior vice president of Morgan Stanley and a partner of The Bach Group, which during his tenure (1993 to 2001) managed more than half a billion dollars for individual investors.

David Bach lives with his wife, Michelle, and son, Jack, in New York, where he is currently working on his eighth book, *Smart Homeowners Finish Rich*. Please visit his web site at **www.finishrich.com**.

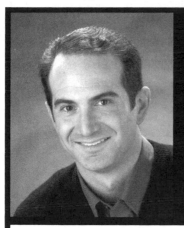

Finishing Rich is as Easy as 1-2-3-! at FinishRich.com

Step 1 Go to our web site at **www.finishrich.com.** There you can join our FinishRich Community by registering for my powerful FREE FinishRich Newsletter. Each month I'll send you my thoughts on the economy as well as useful ideas to help you succeed both personally and financially—AND you'll receive any updates we make to any of the FinishRich books.

Step 2 Attend a FinishRich Live Event in your area. Each month, courses based on my books are taught throughout North America, and 95% of them are FREE. Find the updated listing at www.finishrich.com.

Step 3 Download the FREE *Start Late, Finish Rich* audio program called "The Five Secret Questions to Start Late and Finish Rich." These Five Questions are designed to get you to take immediate action toward realizing your dreams and going for the life that you deserve.

How to Reach Us

Go to **www.finishrich.com** or e-mail us at *success@finishrich.com*. I love hearing about your successes, and I learn from your suggestions and questions. I promise—if you send it, we will read it!

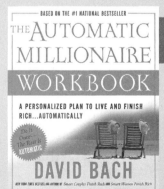
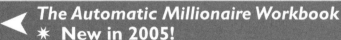

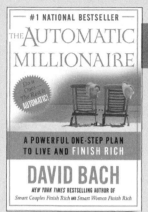
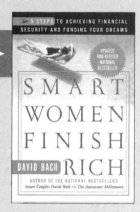
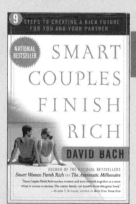

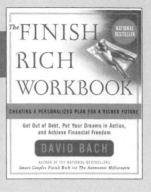
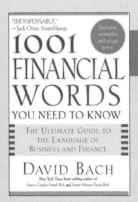

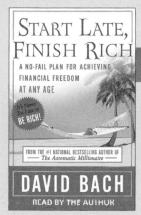

Start Late Finish Rich on Audio CD

Listen to David Bach as he takes the FinishRich wisdom and tailors it specifically to all of us who forgot to save, procrastinated, or got sidetracked by life's unexpected challenges and are now worried that it's too late to achieve financial freedom. Well, David Bach has incredibly good news—it's never too late and in this audio he shows you exactly what to do to get started right away.

The Automatic Millionaire on Audio CD ➤

Now you can listen to the # 1 *New York Times* bestseller on audio CD. Read by David Bach, this one little audiobook has the power to secure your financial future. *The Automatic Millionaire* starts with the powerful story of an average American couple—he's a low-level manager, she's a beautician—whose joint income never exceeds $55,000 a year, who somehow manage to own two homes debt-free, put two kids through college, and retire at fifty-five with more than $1 million in savings. Through their story you'll learn the surprising fact that you cannot get rich with a budget! You must have a plan to pay yourself first that is totally automatic, a plan that will automatically secure your future and pay for your present.

Smart Couples Finish Rich on Audio CD

The second book in the FinishRich series and read by David Bach, this # 1 national bestseller covers:
✓ How to talk about money with your partner without fighting
✓ How to plan your dreams together as a couple
✓ The biggest mistakes couples make with their retirement accounts
✓ The 8 golden rules to hiring a financial advisor
✓ The 10 biggest mistakes couples make financially
✓ How to grow your income by 10% in the next 9 weeks
✓ The CouplesFinishRich quiz: your tool to see how smart you are about money

Available wherever books are sold • www.finishrich.com

The Automatic Millionaire
Home Study Course

In this home study audio program packed with how-to tips, David takes a personal approach to the insights he shared in *The Automatic Millionaire*. You'll be coached by David as though he's in your home, car, or office as he reveals even more strategies, secrets, and tactics to help you turn an ordinary income into a lifetime of financial freedom…easily and automatically. The complete Automatic Millionaire Home Study Course is filled with critical tools and additional information you won't find anywhere else, including:

✓ <u>8 extraordinary audio sessions</u>
✓ <u>An Exclusive Bonus Session: How to Put Your Financial House in Order</u>
✓ <u>Accompanying Workbook on CD-ROM</u>

Best of all, with The Automatic Millionaire Home Study Course, you'll have David Bach as your personal, one-on-one financial coach. Through these audio sessions, he'll be available to you whenever you need him, so you'll never forget your focus or lose momentum. You can check in anytime you want a strategy review, a shot of power, or a fresh dose of inspiration. And you can listen anywhere—while you're commuting, traveling—or even exercising!

Also included in the Automatic Millionaire Home Study Course is a copy of the #1 Bestseller, *The Automatic Millionaire,* and our exclusive Latte Factor Travel Mug.

To order visit www.finishrich.com.

I just wanted to take a minute to tell you how much I enjoyed your book, *The Automatic Millionaire*. I have never been interested in finance, investing, saving, or planning for retirement. In fact, I thought those who took an interest in money matters were self-indulgent, stingy, and shallow.

However, my 50th birthday (!) is only a few years away so "retirement" started to really enter my awareness. I saw you on the *Today* show and thought *The Automatic Millionaire* sounded so easy that maybe even I could do it. A few weeks later I saw the book and purchased it. It was an informative and easy read...and surprisingly uplifting!

In a few short weeks, I've opened an ING Direct account with automatic payroll deductions, increased my employer-matched retirement fund payroll percentage (TIAA-CREF), and made substantial headway in paying off my credit card debt (now at $1,200 and falling rapidly). I'm excited to begin this adventure—thank you!

Tom Mantoni
Eaton, PA

After reading *The Automatic Millionaire*, I called my bank and increased my monthly mortgage payment so that it will end up being more than 2 extra payments per year, automatic, of course. I also called ING Direct and set my savings account on automatic deduction from my bank 2 times per month. My husband called his HR department and increased his 401(k) contributions to 12% per month.

I am 68. Tom is 61. But it's never too late, right? Thanks so much,

Thomas H. Claus and Gail Ingis-Claus
Fairfield, CT

Your book, *Smart Women Finish Rich*, has changed my life. I read it three months ago and since then I have paid down $3,000 in credit card debt, renegotiated the rate on that credit card, established an "Emergency Basket" that already has over $1,000 in it, and opened a Roth IRA to be funded each year. Before reading your book, I had no savings whatsoever and the balance of my credit card was around $4,000. I just want to thank you for teaching me how to fund my future and my dreams!

Christi Dean
Newbury Park, CA

Thank you so much! I always thought I had control and knew what to do with our money, but I really didn't. My wife was only contributing 6% into her 401(k) while I was contributing only 8%. We had all of our savings earning less than 1%. After reading your book, we moved 6 months' worth of joint expenditures into a money market account, earning over 2% (and only going up from here). I upped my 401(k) contribution to 10% and my wife and I opened up 2 separate Roth IRA's for retirement, maxing them out by automatically deducting money every month. We are only 27 years old, we own our own home, and are on our way to financial freedom.

Thank you!

Jim and Kim O'Hara
Melville, NY

Smart Women Finish Rich inspired me in a way you could never imagine. I completed the worksheets, examined my goals, and organized my financial folders. I started a savings account while further reducing my spending. Progress was apparent, but I wanted more! Then I read *The Automatic Millionaire*. Again ... wow! I can do this! Bottom line...entire credit card debt has been paid off, resulting in excellent credit reports. My biweekly mortgage payments are significantly decreasing my principal. I started contributing to a retirement account at work, raising my contributions every time I get a raise (I'm up to 17%). I have an automatic deduction to a savings account as well AND I'm having fun! I have become a certified diver, learned to play golf, and am living life to the fullest. People now ask ME, a single woman, how I do so well financially. I tell everyone about your books and the Latte Factor. I'm such a believer in the principles of your books, I even give *Smart Couples Finish Rich* as an engagement present. Now that's a gift that keeps on giving!

Kathleen Milner
Plymouth, MA

I read *Smart Women Finish Rich* two years ago about the same time my divorce was final. I had some credit card debt, no savings, was not contributing to my 401(k), and was renting a very small house for my daughters and myself. Your book put me on a path to financial independence. Along this path, I have found my self-esteem renewed and my self-confidence returned. It was difficult for me to see past the daily financial struggle of living paycheck to paycheck. With your advice, I have been able to accomplish the following:

- ✓ Organized financial filing system
- ✓ Paid all recurring bills automatically
- ✓ Increased my 401(k) contribution to 12% (company contributes 3%)
- ✓ Purchased a home and refinanced mortgage to a 15-year loan
- ✓ Rolled over two 401(k) plans from previous employers into a traditional IRA
- ✓ Purchased additional life insurance
- ✓ Began taking my daughters on an annual vacation (St. Louis, Chicago, Disney/Orlando)
- ✓ Paid all credit card bills in full each month maintaining a zero balance
- ✓ Purchased a new car, only financing $10,000 over 3 years.

I still have a few things on my "Finish Rich To Do List" but I believe I am definitely on the right path. I must admit that I love the journey and I feel very grateful that you have shared your financial knowledge with me. In turn, I have shared your book with several friends and family members hoping to help others as you have helped me.

Amy Manske
Prairie Village, KS

Your book, *Smart Couples Finish Rich*, was a gift from my Dad and it is changing our lives. My husband and I read the first 100 pages the first few days we had the book. We quickly drew out our value circles (a life-changing exercise in itself) and reorganized our filing system. We have big goals and dreams and in order to get there we have to take care of BIG debts standing in our way but since starting your book, we can see the light! Now more than ever, we are on our way to success. We are thrilled with your ideas and we can't wait to start teaching our son about investing early. Thank you, thank you, thank you!! This is one of the best gifts my Dad could have gotten us.

Michelle Collazo
Tucson, AZ

Your book inspired me to take many steps toward becoming an Automatic Millionaire. In one week I have started paying 10% more on my 15-year mortgage, increased my 403(b) to 10% and consolidated my debt at 0% interest and it is all AUTOMATIC. I feel less stress and anxiety over my financial future.

RJ Sykes
Houston, TX

Following the steps outlined in *Smart Women Finish Rich* inspired me to pay off my debt in its entirety, revamp my ailing credit history and save toward retirement when beforehand, I'd been living paycheck to paycheck for most of my life. Right now I'm experiencing yet another layoff, which before reading your books would have set me back for years. I now have the luxury of choosing from good options and can support myself for a couple of years, if necessary. I'm looking forward to becoming an automatic investor in the near future. Thank you so much for the information and inspirational books.

Kristin Wall
Stockton, CA

On behalf of me and my future wife, I wanted to thank you for making my life automatic. My father has been trying to teach me about money for years but I always thought it was too complicated or that I didn't have the extra income to make a difference. Little did I know that it was so easy. I was a quarter of the way through *The Automatic Millionaire* when I was so moved by your *"How many hours per day do you work for YOURSELF"* formula that I literally got up, went to my computer, and cranked up my 401(k) contribution from 4% to 15%! At the same time I also set up an additional deduction to my savings account. My fiancée and I live the exact same lifestyle as we lived before. However, our lives are richer knowing that there will be a pot of gold waiting for us at retirement. We're also looking to buy our first home next year and it makes it so much easier knowing that the money is there waiting for us. *The Automatic Millionaire* should be mandatory reading for every high school and college student across the country. The information is too good to pass up and it sure as heck beats chemistry. From the bottom of my heart…thank you. You've changed my life.

Chris Kesler
Austin, TX